Chesapeake and Ohio

DINING CAR
RECIPES

COMPILED BY

E. STERLING "TOD" HANGER, JR.

Chesapeake & Ohio Historical Society, Inc.

Acknowledgements

The Society appreciates the assistance provided by the following individuals for contribution of their time, talents, efforts, knowledge and archival materials for use in the production of this book:

James Bernges, Michael Coleman, Eric D. Crane, Thomas W. Dixon, Jr., E. Sterling "Tod" Hanger, Jr., Katie Letcher Lyle, Kenneth L. Miller, David L. Powell, Gertrude Rice, Jessie J. Smith, William R. Sparkmon.

Photo Credits

Unless otherwise indicated, all photographs used in this book are from the Chesapeake & Ohio Historical Society Collection.

Production

This book was designed by Kenneth L. Miller, Miller Design & Photography, Salem, Virginia. The headings are set in New Berolina, body text is Joanna and Joanna Italic.

Foreword

O f the railroad dining car services, Chesapeake & Ohio's was among the most steeped in tradition. Whether this trait was intentional or by happenstance is not fully known. One may surmise the railroad's moderate size and region of passenger train service would account, at least in part, for its casual and Southern-styled traditional approach to service.

The C&O's dining service was born in May of 1889 with the inauguration of a new train called the *Fast Flying Virginian* which traversed the railroad between Cincinnati and New York. Although the dining service on this train was initially operated by The Pullman Company, by 1890 C&O had assumed the entire operation of the diners.

In the study of C&O's dining operations, it would appear there was generally no specifically prescribed way to cook a particular menu item...the dining car cooks were taught by their mentors (under the watchful eye of the steward) aboard their assigned cars in the methods of preparation rather than through an organized classroom style training program. Additionally, while there was at least some overall "style" to their service, dining car wait staff was somewhat similarly coached in the details by the steward of the car to which they were assigned.

Many of those persons who were initially hired by C&O to staff the dining operations spent their entire careers on the diners, thus handing down the traditions, recipes and methods to the "youngsters" as they joined the team aboard their cars. Studying the seniority roster of C&O dining service employees active in 1948, it is readily apparent that there were numerous persons whose longevity dated to the 1910-1920 era. When the C&O inaugurated its famous passenger train *The George Washington* in 1932, there was apparently some organized instruction provided to the crews which staffed the three dining cars assigned to the new train in order to provide consistent food and service in character with its colonial theme.

World War II forced some dramatic changes upon dining services on all the railroads, and C&O's traditional service was not an exception. With the marked increase of passenger traffic in support of the war effort, the diners became almost the equivalent of a mess hall on wheels. Instead of providing the finest "hotel style" foods and service, the railroads were pressed to provide quantity and speed in food service to meet the necessities of the day. Concurrently, the increased need for more and larger trains required the railroads to enlarge their dining operations by adding more dining cars and the crews necessary to operate them. As one can imagine, any semblance of traditional training was no longer practical in this atmosphere and the emphasis became even more directed towards mass feeding.

With the passing of World War II, the railroads redirected their attention to civilian passenger business. C&O was certainly no different and, in fact, became a leader among the nation's railroads in its efforts to develop and operate innovative passenger train equipment, including placement of the largest order for railroad passenger cars ever entered by a single railroad.

Robert R. Young, a noted Wall Street financier and socialite of that era, was chairman of Chesapeake and Ohio during this period of innovation. It was his direct input and determination that led C&O to take the forward jump into post-war passenger service, which was to include a magnificent new streamliner to be called The Chessie (named after C&O's famous mascot "Chessie the Kitten") scheduled to operate between Cincinnati and Washington. This wonderful new train would carry such amenities as hostesses, music piped to each individual seat, theater car, children's playroom, the first dome cars in the east, and myriad additional appointments and services previously unheard of in railroad passenger service. Naturally, new dining cars were among the trains most touted features.

In order to make the dining experience unique, Young decided it would be necessary to retrain the railroad's dining service personnel to ensure consistent food preparation, style and service. To undertake this task, Young enlisted Chef Michael L. DeZutter, "food expert, gourmet and renowned figure in the catering field as manager of the Cloud Club, the Wall Street Club and Blind Brook in New York..." DeZutter, assisted by his associate John Sector, (a Frenchman who had "prepared food for the great and near-great at such New York hotels as the old Waldorf and the new, the Commodore and the Biltmore") began classes for the dining service employees at the railroad's commissary in Cincinnati Union Terminal on July 22, 1947. In preparation for this program, C&O had a complete, operating dining car kitchen installed in the commissary in order to provide a realistic environment in which the employees could practice their skills.

To their credit, DeZutter and Sector both traveled aboard the C&O's diners to observe the crews at work, prior to developing the training course. An article in *Tracks* (C&O's corporate magazine) quoted them as saying "We don't want to tell a chef to make something he is not equipped to prepare. We are simplifying everything to fit the limited space of train kitchens and to utilize the available and recognized talents of our cooks. We want to serve the best food possible - the very finest any cook can turn out - and above all we want a roast of lamb to taste just as good in one of our diners at Richmond, Va., as it does in one of our diners in Detroit or Grand Rapids, Mich."

It was for this effort that the recipes in this book were developed by DeZutter. Mimeographed sheets issued in a small ring-binder to all the C&O chefs, the series of recipes was entitled *It Can Be Done On Wheels*, and is the only known recipe book ever issued or distributed by the C&O to its dining car personnel.

Unfortunately, the train for which this effort was initially targeted - *The Chessie* - never operated. By the time the passenger cars were delivered by the manufacturer, the railroad passenger market had begun a steady decline and C&O sold to other railroads almost all the cars it had purchased for this train. Three of the food service cars built for the train (lunch counter-diner-observation cars 1920, 1921, and 1922) were retained by the C&O and used primarily on *The George Washington* until Amtrak took over the nation's railroad passenger service in 1971 and further served Amtrak for several years thereafter. C&O relied upon its fleet of pre-war heavyweight diners to carry on much of the remaining business of dining service throughout the 1950's and well into the 1960's, finally retiring the heavyweight cars as trains were discontinued during the further decline in passenger operations.

As time passed, the C&O's cooks began to return to some of

their traditional recipes. New recipes were added as the dining car department tried to provide further variety (and economy) to the menus. From 1952 on, the DeZutter inspired recipes were largely set aside and new recipes were generally taken from contemporary magazines or other sources and circulated with any new menu instructions issued to crews by the superintendent of dining services, who was by then based at the commissary in Ashland, Kentucky.

Here then, without any alteration other than enhanced typography and layout— along with a few period photographs — is the C&O's dining car recipe book as issued in 1947. *Bon apetit!*

Tod Hanger
Alderson, West Virginia
January, 1995

Michael L. DeZutter, food authority and consultant to the C&O Dining-Car Department, unveils a culinary secret to this kitchen crew.

NOVEMBER 1947   39

Notes

Introduction

Your employers, The Chesapeake & Ohio Railway Company have, at considerable expense, retained the services of a professional group to teach the stewards, cooks, and waiters, the proper handling of food - its preparation and service.

The course that you will be given will be all-inclusive and it is hoped that pupils will take full advantage of it in order to receive all of the benefits which are intended. It is also hoped that each pupil, of his own free will and accord, will ask any questions that are in his mind. All pupils will be graded according to their initiative and ability. In addition to the benefits resulting from the classes, it is hoped that it will make your work simpler and more enjoyable, yet making you outstanding exponents of your trade in the dining car operation.

Due to the short time allotted for this course, we hope that the pupils will cooperate in every way possible and should it be necessary, we will repeat part of the course at a later date when the full change, namely, menus and type of production, is put in operation.

Cincinnati, Ohio
July, 1947

Weights and Measures

1/2 Pint	1 Cupful
1 Quart	4 Cupsful
3 Teaspoonfuls	1 Tablespoonful
1 Gill	1/2 Cupful
4 Gills	1 Pint
2 Pints	1 Quart
4 Tablespoonfuls	1 Wine-glassful
60 Drops	1 Teaspoonful
4 Wine-glassfuls	1 Cupful
2 Quarts	1 Gallon
2 Tablespoonfuls Sugar	1 Ounce
4 Tablespoonfuls Flour	1 Ounce
2 Tablespoonfuls Butter	1 Ounce
1 Quart Flour	1 Pound
1 Pint Butter	1 Pound
8 Large Eggs	1 Pound
2 Cupfuls Milk	1 Pound
2 Cupfuls Sugar	1 Pound
2 Cupfuls Butter	1 Pound
1 Cupful Crumbs	1/4 Pound
1 Cupful Chopped Suet	1/4 Pound
1 Square Chocolate	1 Ounce
4 Cupfuls Whole Wheat Flour	1 Pound
4-1/2 Cupfuls Graham Flour	1 Pound
1 Cupful Chopped Nut Meats	1/4 Pound
2-2/3 Cupfuls Cornmeal	1 Pound

* - All Measures must be level

Index To Recipes

Varieties Of Seasonings

Sugar, Granulated	Cinnamon Stick
Sugar; XXXX	Cinnamon Powder
Salt	Nutmeg - Whole
Pepper, Black, Whole	Nutmeg - Ground
Pepper, Black, Ground	Ginger Powder
Pepper, Cayenne, Ground	Celery Salt
Cloves, Whole	Bayleaves
Paprika Powder	Thyme - Whole
Curry Powder	Thyme - Ground
Sage, Ground	Coriander Seeds

Notes

RELISHES

Vegetables Grecian Style

(Spiced Vegetables)
Formula No. 1 • Quantity - 80 Portions

Ingredients

2 Heads of Cauliflower, cut in small flowers
4 Pints of mushrooms,
heads and stems cut in quarters, separately
2 Stalks of Celery, cut in 1 inch strips,
1/4 inch wide, well washed
6 Jars of Boiled Small Onions
1-1/2 Gallons of Hot Water
2 Cups of Salad Oil
2 Cups of Tarragon Vinegar
1 Cup of Tomato Paste
5 Tablespoons of Curry Powder
5 Tablespoons of Salt
4 Bayleaves
5 Cloves of Garlic, crushed and chopped
6 Whole Cloves
1 Teaspoon of Thyme Leaves
1 Tablespoon of Coriander Seeds
1 Teaspoon of Whole Pepper
1/2 Cup of Lemon Juice
4 Tablespoons of Freshly Chopped Parsley

Procedure

Place the following ingredients in a piece of cheese cloth -
bayleaves, cloves, thyme, coriander seeds, whole pepper.

Put water in pot bring to a boil add vinegar, add cheese cloth
filled as above. Boil for ten (10) minutes; add cauliflower and
celery, mushrooms, oil, salt, curry powder, garlic, tomato
paste, cook slowly in covered pot until the cauliflower is done
(on the firm side), add onions, bring to a boil, set to cool
without straining. Add lemon juice and chopped parsley and
place in cold box.

When serving, use perforated spoon.

SOUPS

The George Washington

Boston Clam Chowder

Formula No. 101 • Quantity 1 Gallon

Ingredients

30 Chowder Clams
1/2 Gallon of Water
3 Sprigs of Celery
1/2 Cup finely chopped salt pork
2 Cups of Onions, cut in 1/4 inch dice
2 Cups of Celery, cut in 1/4 inch dice
2 Cups of Leeks, cut in 1/4 inch dice
2 Bay leaves
1 Clove of Garlic, chopped fine
1/2 Teaspoon of ground Thyme
4 Cups of raw Potatoes, cut in 1/4" cube
4 Cups of Milk, scalded
1 Tablespoon of Butter
2 Tablespoons of fresh Parsley, chopped
Salt and Pepper to taste

Procedure

Line bottom of pot with sprigs of celery; add clams, (well washed) add water, bring to a boil and remove from fire, strain broth thru fine strainer, remove clams from shell, cut hard tongues and skins off and cut clams in small squares. Put in small bowl, cover with a little broth.

Heat salt pork in pot until half rendered, add onions, celery, leeks, garlic, thyme, bay leaves, simmer slowly for five (5) minutes without coloring. Add clam broth, when boiling add potatoes. Let simmer until vegetables and potatoes are done. Add scalded milk and simmer two (2) more minutes, finish with butter, parsley and clams. Serve with chowder crackers.

Manhattan Clam Chowder

Formula No. 102 • Quantity 1 Gallon

Ingredients

30 Chowder Clams
1/2 Gallon of Cold Water
3 Sprigs of Celery
1/2 Cup of Chopped Salt Pork
1 Cup of Green Peppers, cut in 1/4" dice
2 Cups Whole Onions cut in 1/4" dice
2 Cups of Celery cut in 1/4" dice
2 Cups of Leeks cut in 1/4" dice
2 Bayleaves
1 Clove of Garlic, chopped fine
1/2 Teaspoon of Ground Thyme
1-1/2 No. 2-1/2 Can of Whole Tomatoes
3 Cups of raw Potatoes, cut in 1/4" dice
1 Tablespoon of Corn Starch
1 Tablespoon of Butter
2 Tablespoons of freshly chopped Parsley
Salt and Pepper to taste.

Procedure

Line bottom of pot with sprigs of celery, add clams, well washed, add water bring to a boil and remove from fire, strain broth thru fine strainer, remove clams from shell, cut hard tongues and skins off and cut clams in small squares, put in small bowl, cover with a little broth.

Heat salt pork in pot until half rendered, add green peppers, onions, celery, leeks, garlic, thyme, bayleaves. Simmer slowly for five (5) minutes without coloring, add potatoes and clam broth, when boiling add potatoes. Let simmer until vegetables and potatoes are done. Dilute cornstarch in small quantity of water and simmer three (3) minutes more. Finish with butter and parsley and clams. Serve with chowder crackers.

Cream of Carrots Soup

Ingredients

1/2 Cup of Lard
2 Medium sized Onions, sliced
2 Stems of Celery, sliced
10 Carrots, sliced
2 Bayleaves
1 Pinch of Thyme
1 Clove of Garlic, chopped fine
1 Cup of Flour
1-1/4 Gallons of Hot Water
4 Tablespoons of Chicken Base
1 Tablespoon of Butter
1 Cup of Cream
Salt and Pepper to taste

Procedure

Heat lard in pot, add onion, celery, carrots, bayleaves, thyme and garlic. Smother well without browning, add flour, blend well, cook for two (2) minutes, add hot water, chicken base, cook for thirty-five (35) minutes, strain with pressure thru a fine strainer, add cream and butter, check seasoning.

Cream of Curry Soup

Formula No. 104 • Quantity - 6 Portions

Ingredients

1 Quart of Chicken Broth
1 Large Onion, chopped
1 Heaping teaspoon of Curry Powder
1/2 Pint of heavy Cream
2 Ounces of fresh Mushroom trimmings
1 Tablespoon of Potato Flour
1 Bayleaf
1 Ounce of Chutney, Liquid only
Salt and Pepper

Procedure

Cook onion in butter or lard in deep pan until the Onion is thoroughly heated. Add curry powder and potato flour. Stir well and add hot chicken broth, salt and pepper to taste, bayleaf and mushroom trimmings. Cook for thirty (30) minutes. Strain and add chutney and cream. Cool on ice and serve very cold in cups.

Note: More cream or chicken broth may be added if it is desired thinner or richer.

Cheese Cream Soup

Formula No. 105 • 5 Portions

Ingredients

24 Ounces of Veal Stock
1 Onion, cut up
6 Ounces of light Cream
2 Egg Yolks
4 Tablespoons of grated Parmesan Cheese
2 Tablespoons of Flour
1 Tablespoon of Butter
Salt and pepper to taste
Celery Salt

Procedure

Cook onion in butter without allowing it to take color. Add flour and stir well. Add hot veal stock, stir, and cook slowly for one-half hour. Mix yolks of eggs with part of the cream and stir into the above mixture; add balance of cream, heat but do not allow to boil; add pepper, celery salt and plain salt to taste. Strain thru a fine strainer, add grated cheese, stir well and serve hot.

Note: The addition of chopped chives will add to this dish.

Cream of Chicken Soup

Formula No. 106 • Quantity - 1 Gallon

Ingredients

1/2 Cup of Lard
1 Onion, sliced
2 Stems of Celery, sliced
2 Bayleaves
1 Pinch of Thyme
1 Clove of Garlic, crushed
1 Cup of Flour
1-1/4 Gallons of Hot Water
4 Tablespoons of Chicken Base
1 Cup of Cream
2 Tablespoons of Butter
1 Cup of Chicken, cooked
2 Tablespoons of freshly chopped Parsley
Salt and Pepper to taste

Procedure

Heat lard, add onion, celery, bayleaves, thyme, garlic, cook slowly without allowing to brown for five (5) minutes, add flour, mix well, add water and chicken base, cook for thirty (30) minutes, strain thru fine strainer. Add diced chicken, rice, butter and cream, heat without allowing to boil. Season to taste with salt and pepper and when serving add pinch of chopped parsley to each cup.

Cream of Mushroom Soup

Formula No. 107 • Quantity - 1 Gallon

Ingredients

1/2 Cup of Lard
2 Medium sized Onions, sliced
3/4 Pound of Mushrooms or one No. 2 Can
2 Bayleaves
1 Pinch of Thyme
1 Clove of Garlic, crushed
1 Cup of Flour
1-1/4 Gallons of Hot Water
4 Tablespoons of Chicken Base
1 Cup of Cream
2 Tablespoons of Butter
1 Cup of Cream

Procedure

Heat lard, add onions, bayleaves, thyme, garlic, and stems of mushrooms sliced. Simmer but do not brown add flour, blend well and cook slowly for five (5) minutes, do not allow to brown. Add water, chicken base, simmer for thirty (30) minutes. Strain, slice heads of mushrooms, cook in pan with butter, add cream, heat thoroughly and add to strained soup. Season to taste.

Cream of Onion Soup

Formula No. 108 • Quantity - 1 Gallon

Ingredients

1/2 Cup of Lard
8 Medium sized Onions, sliced
2 Stalks of Celery, sliced
2 Bayleaves
1 Pinch of ground Thyme
1 Clove of Garlic, crushed
1 Cup of Flour
1 Cup of Cream
1-1/4 Gallons of Hot Water
4 Tablespoons of Chicken Base
2 Tablespoons of Chopped Chives
2 Tablespoons of Butter
1 Cup of Chicken, cooked
2 Tablespoons of freshly chopped Parsley
Salt and Pepper to taste

Procedure

Heat lard in pot, add onions, celery, bayleaves, thyme, garlic and cook slowly without browning. Add flour, blend well and cook slowly for five (5) minutes. Add water and chicken base, cook for thirty (30) minutes, strain, add butter, chives and cream, salt and pepper to taste.

French Onion Soup

Formula No. 109 • Quantity - 1 Gallon

Ingredients

1/4 Cup of Butter
1/4 Cup of Lard
10 Medium sized Onions, sliced
2 Bayleaves
3 Cloves of Garlic, crushed
4 Tablespoons of Chicken Base
1-1/4 Gallon of Hot Water
Salt and Pepper to taste
Few Drops of Worcestershire Sauce

Procedure

Heat butter and lard in pot, add onion, cook slowly stirring from time to time until onions are light golden brown. Add garlic and bayleaves, add water and chicken base, cook until done about thirty (30) minutes. Season to taste with salt and pepper, add a few drops of Worcestershire Sauce. Serve with toasted slices of rolls or French bread and grated cheese on top.

Leek and Potato Soup

Formula No. 110 • Quantity - 1 Gallon

Ingredients

1/3 Cup of Lard
1-1/2 Medium sized Onions, sliced thin
6 Medium sized Leeks, white part only, sliced thin
2 Bayleaves
1 Pinch of Ground Thyme
1 Glove of Garlic, chopped
1 1/4 Gallons of Hot Water
4 Tablespoons of Chicken Base
6 Medium sized Potatoes, sliced thin
1 Cup of Cream
2 Tablespoons of Butter
2 Tablespoons of freshly chopped parsley
Salt and Pepper to taste

Procedure

Heat lard, add onions, leeks, bayleaves, thyme, garlic, cook slowly, do not allow to brown. Add water, chicken base and bring to a boil. Add potatoes, cook until potatoes are done, add cream and butter, salt and pepper. When serving add pinch of chopped parsley in each cup.

Philadelphia Pepper Pot
with Dough Drops

Formula No. 111 • Quantity - 1 Gallon

Ingredients

2 Tablespoons of Lard
2 Cups of Onions, cut in 1/4 inch dice
2 Cups of Celery, cut in 1/4 inch dice
3 Cups of Green Peppers, cut in 1/4 inch dice
2 Bayleaves
1 Clove of Garlic, crushed
1 Pinch of Thyme
1 Gallon of Hot Water
4 Tablespoons of Chicken Base
3 Cups of Raw Potatoes, cut in 1/4 inch dice
3 Cups of Tripe, cut in 1/4 inch dice
1/2 Teaspoon of Ground Black Pepper
1/2 Teaspoon of Salt
1 Cup of sifted Flour
1 Cup of Milk
1 Egg
1 Pinch of Ground Nutmeg
Salt and Pepper
2 Tablespoons of Butter
Season to taste

Procedure

Heat lard in pot, add onions, celery, peppers, bayleaves, garlic, thyme, cook slowly until partly done, add water, chicken base, potatoes and tripe. Season with salt and pepper, cook until the potatoes are done. Mix sifted flour with egg, milk, salt and pepper and nutmeg, beat well, put this mixture through a colander or can having 1/2 inch holes, stirring while dropping dough. Cook for two (2) minutes, check seasoning. Add cream, butter ad freshly chopped parsley.

Vichyssoise Soup

Formula No. 112 • Quantity - 1 Gallon

Ingredients

1/3 Cup of Lard
2 Onions, sliced thin
6 Medium sized Leeks, white part only, sliced thin
2 Bayleaves
1 Pinch of Thyme
1 Clove of Garlic, crushed
1 Gallon of Hot Water
4 Tablespoons of Chicken Base
10 Potatoes sliced thin
1 Cup of Cream
2 Cups of Milk
2 Tablespoons of Chopped Chives
Salt and Pepper to taste
Few Dashes of Worcestershire Sauce

Procedure

Heat lard, add onions, leeks, bayleaves, thyme, garlic, cook slowly without browning for five (5) minutes. Add water, chicken base, potatoes, cook until potatoes are done. Strain thru fine strainer, let cool, add cream and milk, mix well. Season to taste with salt and pepper and worcestershire sauce. When serving add generous pinch of chopped chives to each cut.

Can be served hot, when heating do not allow to boil.

Cream of Tomato Soup

Formula No. 113 • Quantity - 1 Gallon

Ingredients

2 Tablespoons of Lard
1 Medium sized Onion, sliced
1 Stem of Celery, sliced
1 medium sized carrot, sliced
2 Bayleaves
1 Pinch of Thyme
1 Clove of Garlic, crushed
1 No. 2-1/2 Can of Whole Tomatoes
2 Cups of Tomato Puree
5 Quarts of Hot Water
4 Tablespoons of Chicken Base
5 Tablespoons of Corn Starch
1 Tablespoon of Butter
1 Cup of Cream
Salt and Pepper to taste

Procedure

Heat lard in pot, add onion, carrot, celery, bayleaves, thyme, garlic, cook slowly for five (5) minutes, add tomato puree, whole tomatoes, hot water, chicken base. Cook slowly for forty (40) minutes, add corn starch diluted in small quantity of cold water. Simmer for five (5) minutes, strain thru fine Chinese strainer, add cream and butter, whip well when adding same. Season to taste. Do not allow to boil after cream has been added.

Old Fashioned Vegetable Soup

Formula No. 114 • Quantity - 1 Gallon

Ingredients

1/2 Cup of lard
2 Cups of Onions, sliced thin and small
2 Cups of Carrots, sliced thin and small
2 Cups of Celery, sliced thin and small
2 Cups of Leeks, sliced thin and small
1 Cup of Cabbage, cut in small squares
2 Bayleaves
1 Pinch of Ground Thyme
1 Clove of Garlic, chopped
1 1/4 Gallon of Hot Water
4 Tablespoons of Chicken base
1 No. 2-1/2 Can Whole Tomatoes
2 Cups of Potatoes, sliced thin and small
2 Cups of Canned Corn
2 Tablespoons of freshly chopped parsley

Procedure

Heat lard in pot, add onions, carrots, celery, leeks, cabbage, bayleaves, garlic and thyme. Let simmer slowly for five (5) minutes, do not allow to burn up. Add water, chicken base, tomatoes, potatoes. Cook until potatoes are done. Add Corn. Bring to a boil, skim off fat settling on top, check seasoning, add parsley.

Curried Chicken Noodle Soup

Formula No. 115 • Quantity - 1 Quart

Ingredients

1 Quart of Milk
1 Package of Lipton Noodle soup or equal
1 Tablespoon of Butter
1/2 Teaspoon of Curry Powder
Salt and Pepper to taste

Procedure

Heat butter in pot, add curry powder. Stir well and add milk, bring to a boil, add package of noodle soup, cook for seven (7) minutes, stirring occasionally. Serve without straining.

Can be served hot or cold.

Scotch Broth

Ingredients

1/2 Cup of Lard
5 Medium sized Carrots, diced small
4 Medium sized Onions, diced small
4 Stem of Celery, diced small
2 Bayleaves
2 Cloves of Garlic, chopped fine
1/2 Teaspoon of Thyme
1 Tablespoon of Corn Starch
1 1/4 Gallon of Mutton or lamb broth
1 1/2 Cup of Pearl Barley
1 Cup of cooked Lamb, diced small
2 Tablespoons of chopped parsley
1 Cup of Cream
1 Tablespoon of Butter
Salt and Pepper to taste

Procedure

Heat lard in pot, add carrots, onions, celery, bayleaves, garlic. Simmer for five (5) minutes, do not allow to brown, add thyme, mutton broth. When boiling add barley, Simmer until barley is cooked, add lamb meat, corn starch diluted in a little cold water. Bring to a boil, add butter and cream, check seasoning. Sprinkle with chopped parsley when serving.

Old Fashioned Split Pea Soup

Formula No. 117 • Quantity - 1 Gallon

Ingredients

1/2 Cup of Lard
2 Medium sized Onions, diced small
2 Medium sized carrots, diced small
2 Stalks of Celery, diced small
2 Bayleaves
2 Cloves of Garlic, chopped fine
4 Cups of Green Split Peas, washed in cold water
1 Gallon of Water
1 Tablespoons of Chicken Base
1 Smoked Ham bone or knuckle
1 Cup of Cream
1 Tablespoon of Butter
Salt and Pepper to taste

Procedure

Heat lard in pan, add onions, carrots, celery, bayleaves, garlic. Simmer for five (5) minutes, do not allow to brown) add water, chicken base, bring to a boil. Add peas and ham bone or knuckle, salt and pepper. Simmer until peas are well done. Check seasoning. Skim well and remove ham bone and bayleaves, do not strain. Add cream and butter. Serve with buttered croutons.

Green Split Pea Soup

Ingredients

1/2 Cup of Lard
2 Medium sized Onions, sliced
2 Medium sized carrots, sliced
3 Stems of Celery
2 Bayleaves
2 Cloves of Garlic, chopped
4 Cups of green split peas, mashed in cold water
1 Gallon of Water
4 Tablespoons of Chicken base
1 Smoked Ham Bone
1 Cup of Cream
1 Tablespoon of Butter
Salt and pepper to taste

Procedure

Heat lard in pan, add onions, carrots, celery, bayleaves, garlic. Simmer for five (5) minutes do not allow to brown, add water, chicken base, bring to a boil. Add peas and ham bone, salt and pepper. Simmer until peas are well done. Check seasoning. Remove ham bone and bayleaves and strain. Add cream and butter. Serve with buttered croutons.

Puree Mongole

Formula No. 119 • Quantity - 1 Gallon

Ingredients

1/2 Gallon of Tomato Soup - Formula No. 113
1/2 Gallon of Green Split Pea Soup - Formula No. 118
1/2 Cup Julienne of Celery
1/2 Cup Julienne of Carrots
1 Teaspoon of Butter
1 Cup of water
1/2 Cup of cooked Green Peas
2 Tablespoons of freshly chopped Parsley
Salt and Pepper to taste

Procedure

Cook julienne of celery and carrots in cup of water and butter. When done drain and add to heated tomato and pea soup. Check seasoning, add peas. Sprinkle with chopped parsley when serving.

Mullagtawny Soup

Ingredients

1/2 Cup of Lard
2 Medium sized onions, sliced
3 Stems of Celery
2 Bayleaves
1 Clove of Garlic, chopped fine
1 Cup of Egg Plant, peeled and sliced small
2 Apples, quartered, peeled and sliced
2 Level Tablespoons of Curry Powder
2 Level Tablespoons of Flour
1 Gallon of hot water
4 Tablespoons of Chicken Base
1 Cup of Tomato Puree
2/3 Cup of Boiled Rice
1 Cup of Light Cream
1 Tablespoon of Butter
Salt and Pepper to taste

Procedure

Heat lard in pot, add onion, celery, bayleaves, garlic. Simmer a few minutes, add egg plant and apple. Stir well and add curry powder, Simmer one (1) minute, add flour, stir well. Add water, chicken base, tomato puree, salt and pepper. Cook slowly for twenty (20) minutes, remove bayleaves, add cream, cooked rice, and butter. Check seasoning.

Cream Of Asparagus Soup

Formula No. 121 • Quantity - 1 Gallon

Ingredients

1/2 Cup of Lard
2 Medium Onions, sliced
2 Stems of Celery, sliced
2 No. 2-1/2 Cans of Asparagus
2 Bayleaves
1 Pinch of Thyme
1 Clove of Garlic, crushed
1 Cup of Flour
1 1/4 Gallons of Hot Water
4 Tablespoons of Chicken Base
4 Tablespoons of Butter
1 Cup of Cream

Procedure

Heat lard in pot, add onions, celery, bayleaves, garlic, thyme; cook slowly, do not allow to brown, when done add flour, blend well. Cook slowly for two (2) minutes, add asparagus, water, asparagus juice, chicken base. Put on fire until sauce boils. Simmer for thirty (30) minutes. Strain thru a fine strainer, add cream and butter. Check seasoning.

Old Fashioned Bean Soup

Formula No. 122 • Quantity - 1 Gallon

Ingredients

1/2 Cup of Lard
2 Medium Onions, diced small
2 Medium Carrots, diced small
2 Stems of Celery, diced small
2 Bayleaves
2 Cloves of garlic, chopped fine
4 Cups of Navy Beans, washed in cold water
1 Gallon of Water
4 Tablespoons of Chicken Base
1 Smoked Ham bone or knuckle
1 Cup of Cream
1 Tablespoon of Butter
Salt and Pepper
4 Tablespoons of freshly chopped Parsley

Procedure

Heat lard in pan, add onions, carrots, celery, bayleaves, garlic; simmer, do not allow to brown; for five (5) minutes, add water, chicken base, bring to a boil, add beans and ham bone and bayleaves, add cream, butter and parsley.

Serve with buttered croutons.

For Puree of Bean Soup - follow same recipe but strain when done.

Minestrone Soup

Formula No. 123 • Quantity - 1 Gallon

Ingredients

1/2 Cup Lard
2 Cups Onions, sliced thin
2 Cups Carrots, sliced thin
2 Cups Celery, sliced thin
2 Cups Leeks, sliced thin
1 Cup Cabbage, cut in small quarters
2 Bayleaves
2 Cloves of Garlic, chopped
1 1/4 Gallon Hot Water
4 Tablespoons Chicken Base
1 Can No. 2-1/2 Whole Tomatoes, cut up
2 Cups Potatoes, diced small
1/2 Pound Frozen, Small Lima Beans
2 Cups Cooked Spaghetti, cut 3/4" long
2 Tablespoons Freshly Chopped Parsley
1 Soupspoon Grated Cheese, per per person

Procedure

Heat Lard in sauce pan, add Onions, Carrots, Celery, Leeks, Cabbage, Bayleaves and Garlic. Let simmer slowly for five (5) minutes. Do not allow to color. Add Water, Chicken Base, Tomatoes, Potatoes and Lima Beans. Bring to a boil and cook until all vegetables are cooked then add Spaghetti. Boil one more minute. Check seasoning.

When serving, sprinkle Parsley in each cup.

Serve Grated Cheese in a small fruit dish.

(It should be left to the patron to add the Cheese at the table, if they like it.)

FISH

Notes

Baked Fish-White Wine Sauce

Formula No. 200 • Quantity - 12 Portions

Ingredients

4 Pounds of Cleaned Filet of Fish
1/4 Cup Shallots or Onion, finely chopped
1 Cup of White Wine
1/2 Cup of Water
Juice of 2 Lemons
2 Tablespoons of Butter
5 Cups of Cream Sauce - Formula No. 901
Salt and Pepper to taste
Freshly chopped parsley or chives

Procedure

Cut fish in portion size, place in buttered shallow baking pan - Sprinkle with shallots, add white wine, water, lemon juice, salt and pepper. Cook in hot oven until done about eight (8) minutes, when done pour liquid from baked fish in sauce pan, cook down until reduced to 1/3 its volume. Add cream sauce, simmer for two (2) minutes, check seasoning, when serving pour sauce over each portion of fish. Sprinkle with chopped parsley.

Cod Fish Cakes

Formula No. 201 • Quantity - 10 Portions, 2 Cakes Each

3 1/2 Pounds of Frozen Filet of Haddock
1-1/2 Pounds of Potatoes (6 Medium Potatoes)
3 Egg Yolks
Salt and Pepper

Procedure

Cook filet of haddock in salt water, drain and remove all bones. Boil potatoes in salt water, drain, mash, keep warm, add yolks of eggs, cook on a slow fire for two (2) minutes, add fish and mix thoroughly, season with salt and pepper to taste. Let cool. Shape in cake form, dip in batter and bread crumbs or cracker meal, fry in shallow pan. Serve with sauce as directed.

Curried Shrimp

Formula No. 202 • Quantity - 6 Portions

Ingredients

2 Tablespoons of Butter
6 Cups of Cleaned, cooked Shrimp
4 Cups of Curry Sauce, Formula No. 911
1/2 Cup of Cream

Procedure

Heat butter in shallow pan, add shrimp heat well, add curry sauce; bring to a boil, check seasoning, add cream. Serve with Steamed Rice.

Shrimp Creole

Formula No. 203 • Quantity - 6 Portions

Ingredients

6 Cups of Cleaned Shrimp
2 Tablespoons of Butter
4 Cups Creole Sauce, Formula No. 902
Salt and Pepper to taste

Procedure

Heat butter in pan, add shrimp, let simmer for two (2) minutes, add Creole Sauce, let come to a boil, serve one cup to a portion with Rice Pilaf, Formula No. 601.

Curried Lobster

Formula No. 204 • Quantity - 6 Portions

Ingredients

2 Tablespoons of Butter
6 Cups of Lobster Meat
4 Cups of Curry Sauce, Formula No. 911
1/2 Cup of Cream
Salt and Pepper to taste

Procedure

Heat butter in pan, add lobster meat well seasoned, add curry sauce, bring to a boil and add cream. Serve with steamed Rice.

Lobster Creole

Formula No. 205 • Quantity - 6 Portions

Ingredients

6 Cups of Cooked Lobster, scalloped
2 Teaspoons of Butter
4 Cups of Creole Sauce Formula No. 902

Procedure

Heat butter in pan, add lobster, add heated creole sauce, check seasoning. Serve with Rice Pilaf.

Shrimp Newburg

Formula No. 206 • Quantity - 6 Portions

Ingredients

6 Cups of cooked and cleaned Shrimps
1 Tablespoon of Butter
1 Teaspoon of Paprika
Salt and Pepper
1 Cup of Cream Sauce - Formula No. 901
2 Raw Egg Yolks
2 Cups of Light Cream
1 Tablespoon of Sherry

Procedure

Heat butter in pan, add shrimp and heat well. Sprinkle with paprika, salt and pepper, add cream sauce. Simmer for five (5) minutes, add egg yolks diluted in a small amount of light cream, heat well until sauce thickens, do not boil and stir well to prevent curdling. Add sherry and serve with Melba Toast or Rice Pilaf.

Lobster Newburg

Formula No. 207 • Quantity - 6 Portions

Ingredients

6 Cups of scalloped Lobster
1 Tablespoon of Butter
1 Teaspoon of Paprika
Salt and Pepper
1 Cup of Cream Sauce - Formula No. 901
2 Raw Egg Yolks
2 Cups of Light Cream
1 Tablespoon of Sherry

Procedure

Heat butter in pan, add lobster and heat well. Sprinkle with Paprika, salt and pepper, add cream sauce. Simmer for five (5) minutes, add egg yolks diluted in a small amount of light cream, heat well until sauce thickens, do not boil and stir well to prevent curdling. Add sherry and serve with Melba Toast or Rice Pilaf.

Lobster a la King

Ingredients

1 Tablespoon of Lard
1 Green Pepper, hulled and sliced fine
1/2 Cup of Red Pimentos, sliced
1 Cup of Mushrooms, Sliced (fresh or canned)
6 Cups of cooked Lobster, scalloped
4 Cups of Cream Sauce, Formula No. 901
2 Tablespoons of Sherry Wine
Salt and Pepper

Procedure

Heat lard in pan, add peppers and mushrooms. Simmer until done, add pimentos, lobster and sherry. Heat and add hot cream sauce. Bring to a light boil. Check seasoning.

Serve with Rice Pilaf.

When canned mushrooms are used cook green peppers first then add mushrooms at same time as pimentos.

Chesapeake Bay Fish Dinner

Formula No. 209 • Quantity - 12 Portions

Ingredients

1 Tablespoon of Butter
12 Portion size cuts of Fish (or 4-1/2 lbs.)
36 Oysters
1/4 Cup of Onions, finely chopped
1/2 Cup of Lemon Juice (2 Lemons)
2 Cups of Water
Salt and Pepper
3 Cups of Cream Sauce, Formula No. 901
36 Parisian Potatoes
(boiled in salt water, kept firm)
36 Small boiled white Onions
2 Tablespoons of Chopped Chives
(if not available use freshly chopped parsley)

Procedure

Place fish in buttered bake pan, setting oysters over fish, sprinkle chopped onion overall, add lemon juice, water, salt and pepper. Bring to a boil and bake in oven for five (5) Minutes. When done drain juice in sauce pan and reduce on top of range to half the amount. Then blend in cream sauce. Bring to a boil, add chives, check seasoning. In serving place one portion of fish in shirred egg dish - arranging 3 Oysters over fish, 3 onions to one side and 3 potatoes on opposite side. Pour cream sauce over all and serve very hot. (Sauce should not be too thick.)

Fish-Pan Fried Or Saute

Ingredients

1/2 Cup of Cream in bowl
Salt and Pepper
1 Cup of Flour in pie pan
Just enough oil to cover bottom of pan
1 Slice of skinned Lemon
A little Brown Gravy and Lemon Juice
Freshly chopped Parsley
1 Teaspoon of Butter to finish

Procedure

Dip fish in cream. Allow excess cream to drip off and lay fish on flour, skin side down. Salt and pepper on top flesh side and turn in flour. Cover well with flour, then shake excess flour and fry to a golden brown in black frying pan on top of range) using small amount of oil. When done, place fish on plate, running a ribbon of brown gravy around fish a little lemon juice over it, topped with a skinned ring of lemon and a little chopped parsley. Then take a teaspoon of butter, place it in pan, allow to brown a little and pour over the whole.

Chesapeake Bay Fish Stew

Formula No. 211 • Quantity - 12 Portions

Ingredients

1 Tablespoon of Butter
12 Portions of Filet of Haddock (4 Oz. each) 3 pounds.
24 Shelled Oysters
1/2 Cup of Onions, chopped fine
1 Pinch of saffron
1/2 Cup of Lemon Juice
1 Cup of Water
36 Shrimps, pre-cooked
2 Cans of Shad Roe or 4 fresh Roe-Pre-Cooked in salt water
3 Cups of Cream Sauce, Formula No. 901
2 Tablespoons of Chopped Chives
(if not available, use freshly chopped parsley)
Salt and Pepper

Procedure

Place haddock in buttered pan, place oysters on top of fish, sprinkle with chopped onions and sprinkle saffron over all, add lemon juice, salt and pepper, bring to a boil and bake in oven for five (5) Minutes. When done add shrimps and shad roe cut in three. Heat in oven until all is hot, drain juice in sauce pan, add boiling cream sauce, add chives or parsley. Check seasoning. Serve in baking or shirred egg dish; 1 piece of each - haddock and shad roe; three shrimps on one side and two oysters on the other side. Cover all with sauce and serve piping hot.

Baked Creamed Fish With Spinach And Potato Border
(Florentine)

Formula No. 212 • Quantity - 12 Portions

Ingredients

1 Tablespoon Butter
12 Portion Size of Haddock
(5 Ounces per portion or 4 pounds)
1 1/2 Cups Water
Salt and Pepper
3 Cups Cream Sauce, Formula No. 924
2 Pounds Frozen Spinach, cooked and finished
1 Batch Duchesse Potatoes, Formula No. 608
6 Tablespoons Grated Cheese

Procedure

Place Fish in buttered bake pan, season with salt and pepper.
Then add Water and cook for five (5) minutes in oven. When
done, drain juice in sauce pan. Place on top of range and
reduce to half the amount. Then blend in Cream Sauce Boil for
two (2) minutes and check Seasoning. For service, place a
small amount of Spinach on a shirred egg dish, enough to
cover bottom of dish. Then place Fish over Spinach and Cream
Sauce over Fish — enough Sauce to cover all. Duchesse
Potatoes, in pastry bag with dented tube, making a nice potato
border around shirred egg dish. Sprinkle one (1) teaspoon
Grated Cheese over all the Cream, as evenly as possible, and
bake in very hot oven until golden brown.

P.S. This dish can be done with left-overs of any White
Poached Fish or Salmon. The only difference is to blend the
Cream Sauce with the Flaked Fish, using 2/3 cup of Fish per
portion and placing the Creamed Fish over the Spinach) and
proceed same as above Formula.

Shad Roe Fritters

Formula No. 213 • Quantity - 30 Fritters, 10 Portions of 3 each

Ingredients

5 Cans of Shad roe or 10 fresh Shad Roes
1 Batch of Fritter Batter - Formula No. 1203

Procedure

Cut each Shad roe in 5 crosswise pieces. Drop in batter, fry in deep fat until well browned. Drain on pan lined with brown paper to absorb excess fat. If fresh Roes are used precook them in salt water and let cool in broth.

Notes

EGGS

THE **F.F.V.** Fast Flying Virginian

Bacon And Potato Omelet

Formula No. 300 • Quantity - 8 Omelets

Ingredients

3 Medium Potatoes
12 Strips of Bacon
1 Tablespoon of Freshly chopped Parsley
24 Eggs

Procedure

Cut potatoes in small dice (1/8 inch square) parboil for three (3) minutes, drain well, cut bacon across in 1/8 inch strips, fry in pan until cooked, drain, saving fat, return fat to pan, heat and add potatoes, cook until golden brown, add bacon and parsley, for each omelet beat 3 eggs well, put in buttered omelet pan, add one eighth part of the bacon and potatoes and parsley mixture, form and serve on hot plate or platter.

Jelly Omelet

Formula No. 301 • Quantity - 1 Portion

Ingredients

3 Eggs
1 Tablespoon of Currant Jelly
1 Teaspoon of Butter
1/2 Teaspoon of powdered sugar
1 Pinch of Salt

Procedure

Beat Eggs well, add pinch of salt, pinch of sugar, cook in omelet pan when formed stuff center with jelly, turn on hot plate or platter, form properly, sprinkle with powdered sugar. Mark crosswise with hot iron.

Poached Eggs Benedict

Formula No. 302 • Quantity - 1 Portion

Ingredients

2 Eggs
1 English Muffin
1 Breakfast size slice of Ham
Hollandaise Sauce to cover - Formula 903

Procedure

Poach Eggs, split and toast English Muffin. Broil Ham. To Serve: Put half slices of ham on each half of muffin, put one poached egg on each. Cover with Hollandaise Sauce. Serve on hot dinner plate.

Creamed Sliced Eggs And Onions On Toast

Formula No. 303 • Quantity - 10 Portions, 3 Eggs per portion

Ingredients

50 Eggs, hard boiled
12 Medium onions, sliced thin
5 Tablespoons of Butter
5 Cups of Cream Sauce - Formula No. 901
1 Cup of light Cream
5 Tablespoons of freshly chopped Parsley
Salt and Pepper

Procedure

Heat butter in pan, add onions, cook slowly until half done without letting them brown. Add cream sauce, cook until onions are done; stirring from time to time. Add hard boiled eggs put thru egg slicer, add cream and bring to a boil. Season to taste. Serve on dry toast in shirred egg dish; three eggs to a portion. Sprinkle with chopped parsley.

General Information As To -

Breading of Chicken, Veal Cutlet, Lamb Chops,
Pork Tenderloin, Pork Chops, Filet of Fish, Scallops,
Oysters, Clams, Croquettes, Fish Cakes, Etc.

For all the above, proceed with regular breading operation,
which is to season meat, dredge in flour. Then place in Egg
Wash allowing flour to dissolve, forming a sort of batter. Take
out of Egg Wash, allow excess wash to drip off, and place in
bread crumbs, burying well and patting to assure a solid covering. Fry in hot, deep fat. Place in pan lined with brown paper
so as to absorb hot fat dripping from fried item.

Veal Cutlet should be fried in shallow pan on top of stove.

Pork Chops and Lamb Chops should be browned only in
shallow pan and finished in oven to assure cooking through.

MEATS & STEWS

Beef Goulash

Formula No. 400 • Quantity - 24 Portions

Ingredients

1/2 Cup of Lard
12 Pounds boiled and trimmed beef, cut in 1-1/2 inch squares
6 Medium sized onions, diced fine
5 Bayleaves
2 Cloves of Garlic, chopped fine
1/2 Teaspoon ground Thyme
1 Teaspoon Caraway Seeds
3 Tablespoons powdered paprika
2 No. 2 1/2 Cans Whole Tomatoes
1 Cup of Tomato Puree
5 Cups of Water
1 Tablespoon Chicken Base
Salt and Pepper to taste

Procedure

Heat lard in pan, when very hot add meat, brown well, add onions, bayleaves, garlic, thyme, caraway seeds, paprika, blend well, simmer for five (5) minutes, add whole tomatoes, tomato puree, water, chicken base, salt and pepper to taste, bring to a boil, cover and cook in oven until meat is done. Check seasoning. Serve with Noodles, Rice Pilaf or Spatzli.

It is important that all fat be skimmed off.

Curried Veal

Formula No. 401 • Quantity - 24 Portions

Ingredients

1/2 Cup of Lard
12 Pounds of Veal, boned, cut in 1-1/2 inch squares
6 Medium Onions, cut in small dice
3 Bayleaves
2 Cloves of Garlic, crushed and chopped
1 Teaspoon of Thyme
3 Tablespoons of Curry Powder
1 No. 2-1/2 Can of Whole Tomatoes
4 Cups of Water
1 Teaspoon of Chicken Base
1 Cup of Grated Coconut
1 Tablespoon of Corn Starch
1 Cup of Apple Sauce
Salt and Pepper to Taste

Procedure

Heat lard in pan, add veal, let brown. Add onions, garlic, bayleaves, thyme, salt and pepper, blend well, add curry powder, allow sauce to blend well, add tomatoes, water, chicken base, coconut, check seasoning. Bring to a boil, cover and cook in oven until meat is done, add applesauce and corn starch, diluted in cold water, simmer two (2) minutes, remove bayleaves and skim off all fat.

Serve with steamed rice and chutney.

Formula No. 402 • Quantity - 6 a la carte Portions

Ingredients

1/2 Pound ground Fresh Beef Suet
1-1/2 Pound Ground Fresh Lean Beef
1 Medium Onion, Chopped fine
1/2 Cup of Very Cold Water
Salt and Pepper to taste

Procedure

Mix suet and beef, add onions, salt and pepper and mix thoroughly, add cold water slowly. For portions measure in cup not quite full. Shape in oblong shape, 1 inch thick, cook in hot shallow pan in oleo or bacon fat or lard, on fast fire. Keep rare unless otherwise requested.

If you wish to broil same, turn the shaped hamburger in small amount of oil before putting on the broiler.

Irish Lamb Stew

Formula No. 403 • Quantity - 24 Portions

Ingredients

12 Pounds boned Shoulder of Lamb, cut in 1 1/2 inch cubes
8 Medium sized Onions, sliced
10 Medium sized Potatoes, sliced
2 Bayleaves
1 Pinch of ground thyme
2 Cloves of Garlic, crushed
Water to cover
2 Tablespoons of freshly chopped Parsley
Salt and Pepper

Procedure

Par boil meat in boiling water for five (5) minutes. Drain out meat in colander, put meat in suitable size pot, add onions, potatoes, bayleaves, garlic,thyme, salt and pepper, cover with cold water. Cook until meat is done. When serving sprinkle chopped parsley on each portion.

Dumplings, Formula No. 1208, may be served with above.

It is important that all fat be skimmed off.

Lamb Goulash

Formula No. 404 • Quantity - 24 Portions

Ingredients

12 Pounds of Lamb Meat, boned, cut in 1 1/2 inch cubes
1/2 Cup of Lard
6 Medium sized Onions, diced fine
5 Bayleaves
2 Cloves of Garlic, crushed and chopped
1/2 Teaspoon of ground Thyme
1 Teaspoon of Caraway Seeds
5 Tablespoons of Ground Paprika
2 No. 2-1/2 Cans of Whole Tomatoes
1 Cup of Tomato Puree
5 Cups of Water
1 Tablespoon of Chicken Base
Salt and Pepper

Procedure

Heat lard in pan, when very hot, add lamb; brown well, add onions, bayleaves, garlic, thyme, caraway seeds, paprika, let simmer a few minutes, stir well and add whole tomatoes, tomato puree, water, chicken base, salt and pepper; bring to a boil) cover and cook in oven until meat is done, check seasoning. Skim off all fat. Serve with noodles, Elbow Macaroni, Rice Pilaf, or Spatzli.

Spring Lamb Stew With Vegetables

Formula No. 405 • Quantity - 24 Portions

Ingredients

12 Pounds of Boned Shoulder of Lamb,
cut in 1-1/2 inch cubes
1/2 Cup of Lard
2 Medium Onions, chopped fine
2 Bayleaves
2 Cloves of Garlic, chopped fine
1 Pinch of Ground Thyme
2 No. 2-1/2 Cans of Whole tomatoes
6 Cups of Water
Salt and Pepper
8 Medium Carrots, cut in 1 inch cubes
8 Medium Potatoes, cut in 1 inch cubes
2 No. 2 Cans of Boiled small white Onions
1 Tablespoon of Corn Starch
1 No. 2-1/2 Can of Small Green Peas
2 Tablespoons of freshly chopped Parsley

Procedure

Heat lard in shallow pan, add meat, cook until well brown. Transfer meat to deep stew pan using skimmer (save fat in pan). Add chopped onions, bayleaves, garlic, thyme to meat, cook slowly for five (5) minutes, add tomatoes, water and seasoning. (must be fully covered with liquid). Bring to a boil, skim. Cover with lid and cook in hot oven for twenty-five minutes. Take pan with saved fat, place back on fire and add carrots, cook slowly for five (5) minutes without browning. Remove with skimmer and add to stew with potatoes. Return stew to oven and cook until meat is done. Take out and add boiled onions, bring to a boil, skim excess fat, add corn starch diluted in cold water, boil for two (2) minutes, check seasoning. When serving top with tablespoon of cooked peas and sprinkle with parsley.

Veal Goulash

Ingredients

12 Pounds of boned Veal, cut in 1-1/2 inch cubes
1/2 Cup of Lard
6 Medium sized Onions, diced fine
5 Bayleaves
2 Cloves of Garlic, crushed and chopped
1/2 Teaspoon of ground Thyme
1 Teaspoon of Caraway Seeds
5 Tablespoons of powdered Paprika
2 No. 2-1/2 Cans of Whole Tomatoes
1 Cup of Tomato Puree
5 Cups of Water
1 Tablespoon of Chicken Base
Salt and Pepper

Procedure

Heat lard in pan, when very hot add meat, let brown well, add onions, bayleaves, garlic, thyme) caraway seeds, simmer for a few minutes, stir well, add paprika, whole tomatoes, tomato puree, water, Chicken base, salt and pepper. Cover and cook in oven until meat is cooked; check seasoning. Serve with noodles, elbow macaroni, Rice Pilaf or Spatzli. Fat must be skimmed off.

Elbow Macaroni Ham

Formula No. 407 • Quantity -12 Portions

Ingredients

1 Pound of Elbow Macaroni
4 Cups of scalloped or diced cooked lean ham trimming
1 Tablespoon of Butter
3 Cups of Cream Sauce, Formula No. 901
1 Cup of Milk
1 Pinch of grated Nutmeg
4 Tablespoons of grated Cheese
Salt and Pepper

Procedure

Place elbow macaroni in boiling salted water, cook until done, drain, and wash with hot water, put butter in pan, add ham, hock slowly for a few minutes, add cream sauce and milk; bring to a boil, add cooked macaroni, heat thoroughly, add nutmeg, salt and pepper, mix lightly. To Serve - put each portion in shirred egg dish, sprinkle with cheese, bake in hot oven until golden brown.

Noodles or broken macaroni can be used as stated on menu.

Beef Stew Home Style

Formula No. 408 • Quantity - 24 Portions

Ingredients

3 Tablespoons of Lard
12 Pounds of boiled Beef Chuck, cut in 1-1/2 inch cubes
5 Medium sized Onions, sliced
10 Medium sized Carrots; cut in 1 inch cubes
8 Medium sized Potatoes; cut in 1 inch cubes
4 Bayleaves
1/2 Teaspoon of Ground Thyme
3 Cloves of Garlic, crushed
2 No. 2-1/2 Cans of whole Tomatoes
5 Cups of Water
1 Tablespoon of Corn Starch
1 No. 2 -1/2 Can of Fine Peas
2 Tablespoons of freshly chopped Parsley

Procedure

Heat lard very hot, in large pot, add meat; let brown well, then and onions, bayleaves, thyme, garlic, simmer a couple of minutes and add tomatoes, water, salt and pepper, bring to a boil, cover and cook in oven for one hour, add carrots which have been slightly browned in small quantity of lard. Add potatoes, cook until done, skim off all fat, check seasoning, sprinkle peas on top. When serving sprinkle with chopped Parsley

Use same formula for Lamb or Veal - Substituting meats.

Ham And Mushrooms On Toast

Formula No. 409 • Quantity 1 Portion

Ingredients

1 Slice of Ham (Breakfast Size)
7 Heads of Mushrooms
1 Slice of Bread, trimmed square
1 Teaspoon of Butter
Salt and Pepper
1 Pinch of freshly chopped Parsley
1 Teaspoon of Lemon Butter, Formula No. 904

Procedure

Heat butter in pan, add mushrooms, season to taste with salt and pepper, cook until done. Broil ham, toast bread. To serve put ham on toasted bread, arrange mushrooms on top, pour juice remaining from the cooked mushrooms, pour lemon butter on top. Sprinkle with chopped parsley. Serve very hot.

Meat Loaf

Formula No. 410 • Quantity - 10 Portions

Ingredients

2 1/2 Pounds finely ground meat
2 Onions, chopped-fine
1/4 Cup chopped parsley
2 Raw Eggs
4 Slices of white bread soaked in 1/2 cup of milk
1 Tablespoon of Lard
1 Pinch of Ground Nutmeg
Salt and Pepper to taste

Procedure

Heat lard in small pan, add onions, simmer without allowing to brown, put meat in bowl, add cooked onion, parsley, eggs, bread, nutmeg, salt and pepper to taste. Mix well until all ingredients form into loaf using cold water to smooth the sides and top, place in baking pan. roast slowly keep it from getting brown. Serve with family gravy, Formula No. 910.

Braised Beef A La Mode

Formula No. 411 • Quantity - 12 Portions

Ingredients

4 Pounds of boned Beef
1/2 Cup of Lard
1 Carrot, sliced
1 Onion, sliced
1 Stem of Celery, sliced
2 Bayleaves
1/2 Teaspoon of ground Thyme
2 Cloves of Garlic, crushed
1 No. 2-1/2 Can Whole Tomatoes
About 7 Cups of Water, to cover meat
Salt and pepper
3 Carrots, cut in sticks, 1 inch long, 1/4 inch thick
1 White Turnip, medium size, cut same as carrots
1 Tablespoon Corn Starch
24 Small White Boiled Onions
1 No. 2-1/2 Can of Green Peas, cooked
2 Tablespoons of freshly chopped Parsley

Procedure

Heat lard in deep pan, add beef, sear properly all around until brown, add sliced carrots, onions, celery, garlic, thyme, bayleaves, let simmer a few minutes, add tomatoes, water, season with salt and pepper. Bring to a boil, cover and cook in oven for 1-1/2 hours. Transfer meat to other pan, strain gravy over meat, add raw carrot and turnip sticks, cover and return to oven until meat and vegetables, are done, remove meat, skim off all fat, thicken with corn starch diluted in cold water, add cooked onions and peas, heat well. For service slice meat and cover with gravy and vegetables.

Jellied Beef A La Mode

Formula No. 412 • Quantity - 12 Portions

Ingredients

(Same as Braised Beef a la Mode)
(Formula No. 411)

Procedure

Prepare quantity of Beef a la mode; formula No. 411, when done add 1/2 teaspoon powdered gelatin diluted in a little sherry wine, let come to a boil, withdraw meat, slice in portions and put each portion in oval baking dish) cover with gravy and vegetables and let cool. Serve very cold.

Yankee Pot Roast

Formula No. 413 • Quantity - 12 Portions

Ingredients

1/2 Cup of Lard
4 Pounds of Boned Beef
1 Carrot, sliced
1 Onion, sliced
1 Stem of Celery, sliced
2 Bayleaves
1-1/2 Teaspoon of ground Thyme
2 Cloves of Garlic, crushed
1 No. 2-1/2 Can of Whole Tomatoes
Salt and Pepper
7 Cups of water, to cover meat
1 Tablespoon of Corn Starch

Procedure

Heat lard in deep pan, add beef, sear well all around, add carrot, celery, onion, bayleaves, thyme, garlic, let simmer a few minutes, add tomatoes, water, salt and pepper, bring to a boil, cover and cook in oven until done. Skim off all fat. When done remove meat, thicken gravy with corn starch diluted in a small quantity of cold water, strain over meat. When serving slice meat and cover with fair amount of gravy.

Veal Fricassee

Formula No. 414 • Quantity - 24 Portions

Ingredients

12 Pounds boned Veal, cut in 1-1/2 squares
2 Medium Onions, sliced
2 Carrots, sliced
2 Bayleaves
2 Cloves of Garlic, crushed
6 Whole Cloves
1/2 Teaspoon of Leaf Thyme
2 Sprigs of Celery, Green
6 Stems of Parsley
4 Tablespoons of Butter
2 Egg Yolks
1/2 Cup of Cream
Salt and Pepper to taste
2/3 Cup of Flour

Ingredients for Garnish

50 Small Boiled Onions
1 No. 2 Can of Peas
2 Tablespoons of freshly chopped Parsley

Procedure

Put meat in pan with cold water to cover bring to a boil, skim well, add carrots, sliced onions, bayleaves, garlic, cloves, thyme, Celery, parsley stems, salt and pepper. Cook until meat is done. Remove meat with skimmer, place in sauce pan, be sure to remove all vegetables and spices used in cooking. Strain broth. Put butter in pan, heat well, add flour, cook for a few minutes, do not allow to color. Add two (2) Quarts of veal broth, cook for fifteen (15) minutes, beat egg yolks with cream and add to sauce, blending well. Add cooked onions and peas, simmer for two (2) minutes, add to pan over veal. When serving sprinkle with chopped parsley. Serve with Rice Pilaf or Noodles.

Oxtail Stew-Home Style

Formula No. 415 • Quantity - 17 Portions
Cooking time 3-1/2-4 hours

Ingredients

1/2 Cup of Lard
12 Lbs. Oxtails, cut in 2 inch cuts
2 Onions Chopped Fine
10 Carrots, cut in 1 inch squares
4 Bayleaves
2 Cloves of Garlic chopped
2 Cans of No. 2-1/2 whole tomatoes
1/2 Teaspoon of ground thyme
2 Cans of No. 2 White, small Onions
Salt and Pepper
2 Tablespoons of freshly chopped parsley
Water to cover

Procedure

Heat 1/4 cup lard in roasting pan. Add oxtails and simmer slowly for fifteen (15) minutes. Add chopped onions. Let color lightly. Add tomatoes, bayleaves, thyme, garlic. Salt and pepper to taste; water to cover. Bring to a boil. Cover and cook in hot oven for 2-1/2 hours. Add 1/4 cup of lard in pan, add carrots. Color lightly add to oxtail stew. Cook until all is well cooked (meat should come off of bones easily). Add small white onions, bring to a boil and skim off excess fat before serving. Sprinkle with freshly chopped parsley.

Potted Swiss Steak

Formula No. 416 • Quantity - 20 Portions

Ingredients

1 Cup of Lard
20 Round Steaks, 7 Oz. each
2 Cups of Flour
4 Medium sized Onions; sliced
2 #2-1/2 Cans of Whole Tomatoes
2 Bayleaves
Water to Cover
Salt and Pepper to taste
2 Tablespoons of freshly chopped Parsley

Procedure

Heat lard in pan, season and dredge steak in flour, put in pan and fry on both sides until golden brown, line up in baking pan, add sauteed onions, tomatoes, water, salt and pepper, bayleaves, bring to a boil, cover and cook in oven until done. Remove bayleaves, check gravy and seasoning, skim off all fat. When serving, sprinkle with chopped parsley.

Cooked Meat Stuffing

Formula No. 417 • Quantity - Stuffing for 24 Peppers

Ingredients

3 Tablespoons of Lard
2 Medium sized Onions, chopped
4 Bayleaves
2 Cloves of garlic, chopped
10 Cups of finely chopped cooked meat (left overs)
2 Cups of Family Gravy - Formula No. 910
1 1/2 Cups of Tomato Puree
Salt and Pepper to taste
Pinch of Ground Nutmeg

Procedure

Heat lard in pan, add onions, cook slowly, do not alloy to brown, add bayleaves, tomato puree, family gravy, nutmeg, garlic, bring to a boil, add meat. Season with salt and pepper, cover and cook in oven for twenty (20) minutes, let cool, and use to stuff peppers, cucumbers, egg plants.

Baked Boston Pork and Beans

Formula No. 418 • Quantity - 12 Portions

Ingredients

2 No. 2 Cans Gibbs Baked Beans
1 Cup fat back, diced fine
1 Medium sized onion, diced fine
2 Bayleaves
1 Clove of Garlic, chopped fine
1 1/2 Cup of Tomato Puree
1 Teaspoon dry Coleman Mustard
3 Tablespoons Molasses
2 Tablespoons Sugar
Salt and Pepper
12 Slices of Cooked Salt Pork (About 1-1/2 to 1-3/4 pounds)
1/4 Teaspoon Lea & Perrins Worcestershire Sauce.

Procedure

Heat diced fat back in pan, add onions, garlic, bayleaves, simmer slowly, do not allow to brown; when onions are done add tomato puree, heat thru, mix mustard, molasses, sugar and worcestershire sauce. Add to above sauce, bring to a boil, add beans, heat well, check seasoning. Check seasoning. Set in deep dish, arrange sliced cooked salt pork on top, sprinkle with a little sugar; bake in fast oven, until pork is nice and brown.

Curried Pork

Ingredients

1/2 Cup of Lard
12 Pounds of Pork, boned, cut in 1-1/2 inch squares
6 Medium Onions, cut in small dice
3 Bayleaves
2 Cloves of Garlic, crushed and chopped
1 Teaspoon of Thyme
3 Tablespoons of Curry Powder
1 No. 2-1/2 Can of Whole Tomatoes
4 Cups of Water
1 Teaspoon of Chicken Base
1 Cup of Grated Coconut
1 Tablespoon of Corn Starch
1 Cup of Apple Sauce
Salt and Pepper to taste

Procedure

Heat lard in pan, add pork, let brown. Add onions, garlic, bayleaves, thyme, salt and pepper) blend well, add curry powder, allow sauce to blend well, add tomatoes, water, chicken base) coconut, check seasoning. Bring to a boil, cover and cook in oven until meat is done, add apple sauce and corn starch, diluted in cold water, simmer two (2) minutes, remove bayleaves and skim off all fat. Serve with steamed rice and chutney.

Stuffed Green Peppers

Formula No. 420 • Quantity - 8 Portions

Ingredients

16 Medium sized peppers
1 Tablespoon of Lard
1 Pound of finely ground Beef
1 Pound of finely ground Pork
3 Medium sized Onions, chopped fine
2 Bayleaves
1 Clove of Garlic, chopped and crushed
1/2 Cup of Tomato Puree
1 Pinch of ground Nutmeg
2 Tablespoons of freshly chopped Parsley
1 1/2 Cups of Cracker Meal
1 Cup of Boiled Rice
Salt and Pepper

Procedure

Heat lard in sauce pan, add ground pork, cook slowly for five (5) minutes, add beef, onions, bayleaves, garlic, thyme, mix well and cook for five (5) minutes, add tomato puree, nutmeg and parsley. Simmer a few minutes, add cracker meal and boiled rice, remove from fire, salt and pepper to taste. Fill whole pepper bells from which you have removed seeds and top. Place peppers in greased pan and cover with greased paper and bake in oven until done (Peppers should be slightly firm.) Serve with Tomato Sauce. Two peppers per portion.

Curried Beef

Ingredients

1/2 Cup of Lard
12 Pounds of Beef, boned, cut in 1-1/2 inch squares
6 Medium Onion, cut in small dice
3 Bayleaves
2 Cloves of Garlic, crushed and chopped
1 Teaspoon of Thyme
3 Tablespoons of Curry Powder
1 No. 2-1/2 Can of Whole Tomatoes
4 Cups of Water
1 Teaspoon of Chicken Base
1 Cup of Grated Coconut
1 Tablespoon of Corn-Starch
1 Cup of Apple Sauce
Salt and Pepper to Taste

Procedure

Heat lard in pan, add veal, let brown. Add onions, garlic, bayleaves, thyme, salt and pepper, blend well, add curry powder, allow sauce to blend well, add tomatoes, water, chicken base, coconut, check seasoning. Bring to a boil, cover and cook in over until meat is done, add applesauce and corn starch diluted in cold water, simmer two (2) minutes, remove bayleaves and skim off all fat. Serve with steamed rice and chutney.

Curried Lamb

Formula No. 422 • Quantity - 24 Portions

Ingredients

1/2 Cup of Lard
12 Pounds of Lamb, boned, cut in 1-1/2 inch squares
6 Medium Onions, cut in small dice
3 Bayleaves
2 Cloves of Garlic, crushed and chopped
1 Teaspoon of Thyme
5 Tablespoons of Curry Powder
1 No. 2-1/2 Can of Whole Tomatoes
4 Cups of Water
1 Teaspoon of Chicken Base
1 Cup of Grated. Coconut
1 Tablespoon of Corn Starch
1 Cup of Apple Sauce
Salt and Pepper to Taste

Procedure

Heat lard in pan, add lamb, let brown. Add onions, garlic, bayleaves, thyme, salt and pepper, blend well, add curry powder allow sauce to blend well, add tomatoes, water, chicken base, coconut, check seasoning. Bring to a boil, cover and cook in oven until meat is done, add apple sauce, and cornstarch, diluted in cold water, simmer two (2) minutes; remove bayleaves and skim off all fat. Serve with steamed rice and chutney.

Fresh Pork Chow Mein

Formula No. 423 • Quantity - 14 to 16 Portions

Ingredients

1/2 Cup Lard
2 Pounds Fresh Pork Shoulder
Cut in strips 1 1/2 inches long and 1/2 inch thick
2 Bayleaves
1 Pinch Ground thyme
1 Clove of Garlic, chopped
4 Medium Onions, sliced
2 Quarts Chop Suey Vegetables
Water
1 Tablespoon Chicken Base
2 Tablespoons Corn Starch
A few dashes of soy sauce
Salt and Pepper

Procedure

Heat lard in sauce pan, when very hot add pork, allow pork to brown up lightly, then add Bayleaves, thyme and Garlic. Toss together for a minute and add onion, simmer for five minutes and add Chop Suey vegetables and enough water to cover the whole, bring to a boil and simmer on side of range until meat and vegetables are done. Thicken with diluted cornstarch and season with soy sauce, salt and pepper. (Soy sauce flavor should dominate slightly. Serve with about a demitasse cup of steamed rice). Chow Mein should not be soupy.

Notes

POULTRY & GAME

The George Washington

Baked Chicken Hunter Style

Formula No. 500 • Quantity - 2 Portions

Ingredients

1 Two (2) Pound broiler, disjointed in four parts
2 Tablespoons of Lard
6 Mushrooms, sliced
1 Ounce of White cooking Wine or Newburg Sauce Wine
1 Pinch of freshly chopped Parsley
1 Cup of Italian Sauce, Formula No. 908

(Cooking time twenty-five (25) minutes)

Procedure

Heat lard in skillet, add chicken, fry to a golden brown until done, add sliced mushrooms, cook for three (3) minutes, add wine; simmer for two (2) minutes. Add Italian Sauce, simmer for a few minutes. Serve one leg and one breast per portion, cover with sauce, sprinkle with parsley.

Creamed Chicken (or Capon) Au Gratin

Formula No. 501 • Quantity - 7 Portions

Ingredients

6 Cups of cooked, boned, diced Chicken
4 Cups of Cream Sauce, Formula No. 901
6 Teaspoons of Butter
1 Egg Yolk
1/2 Cup of Milk
2 Tablespoons of Sherry Wine
Salt and Pepper to taste
6 Teaspoons of grated cheese

Procedure

Heat butter in pan, add chicken, heat well, add Cream Sauce, season to taste, bring to a boil, mix egg yolks with milk, beat well, stir into creamed chicken, do not allow to boil, add sherry wine. Put in portions in individual baking dish, sprinkle with cheese and a few drops of melted butter, bake until golden brown.

Curried Chicken or Turkey

Formula No. 502 • Quantity - 12 Portions

Ingredients

2 Tablespoons of Butter
6 Cups of Chicken or Turkey, scalloped
4 Cups of Curry Sauce, Formula No. 911

Procedure

Heat butter in shallow pan, add curry sauce, bring to a boil, check seasoning. Serve with Steamed Rice.

Fried Chicken Southern Style

Formula No. 503 • Quantity - 12 Portions

Ingredients

1/2 Cup of Lard or Bacon Fat
6 Broilers, 2 pounds each
2 Eggs
1 Cup of Flour
Salt and Pepper

Procedure

Disjoint chicken in four parts each, 2 breasts, 2 legs, remove bone from second joint. Season with salt and pepper, dip in well beaten eggs, pass through flour. Fry in lard or bacon fat in shallow pan slowly until done. Must be golden brown. Serve with Sour Cream Gravy, Formula No. 907.

Minced Chicken (or Turkey) A La King

Formula No. 504 • Quantity - 6 Portions

Ingredients

1 Tablespoon of Lard
6 Cups of Scalloped, boned Chicken or Turkey
1 Green Pepper, sliced
1 Cup of Mushrooms, sliced
4 Cups of Hot Creme Sauce, Formula No. 901
1/2 Cups of Red Pimento, sliced
1/4 Cup of Sherry Wine
Salt and Pepper

Procedure

Heat lard in pan, add mushrooms, green pepper; simmer for five (5) minutes, add scalloped chicken or turkey, sherry wine, pimentos and hot Creme Sauce, bring to a boil, season to taste. Serve with Melba toast or Rice Pilaf.

Spring Chicken Fricassee

Formula No. 505 • Quantity - 20 Portions

Ingredients

10 Broilers, 2 lbs. each, dissected in 4 parts each,
two breasts and two legs
1 Cup of Lard
2 Medium Onions, sliced fine
3 Bayleaves
2 Cloves of Garlic, chopped fine
1 Pinch ground cloves
1/2 Teaspoon of ground Thyme
4 Tablespoons of Butter
2/3 Cup of Flour
2 Quarts of Water
2 Egg Yolks
1/2 Cup of Cream
20 Heads of Mushrooms
1-1/2 Small white Onions, Cooked
1-1/2 Pounds lean, cooked, salt pork, cut in pieces 1 inch long,
1/2 inch wide

Procedure

Heat lard in saute pan, add chicken, cook slowly and allow to color very slightly all over; add onions, let simmer for five (5) minutes, sprinkle with flour, stir well on side of range until flour is well mixed with Chicken, add water, bayleaves, garlic, ground cloves, thyme, salt and pepper, bring to a boil, stirring constantly, cover and cook slowly until chicken is done. Heat butter in pan, add mushrooms, let cook until done, add cooked onions and cooked salt pork, heat well and add to chicken, simmer for five (5) minutes. Mix cream with egg yolks, beat well, pour in fricassee) let come to a boil stirring well. Serve 1 piece of light and 1 piece dark meat with garnish for each portion, sprinkle with chopped parsley, serve with Rice Pilaf.

Curried Minced Chicken

Formula No. 506 • Quantity - 6 Portions

Ingredients

2 Tablespoons of Butter
6 Cups of Scalloped Chicken
4 Cups of Curry Sauce, Formula No. 911
1/2 Cup of light cream
Salt and Pepper

Procedure

Heat butter in pan; add chicken, simmer for a few minutes, add heated Curry Sauce, bring to a boil, cook for five (5) Minutes, add cream. Check Seasoning.
Serve with Boiled Rice; Indian Style.

Minced Chicken Creole

Formula No. 507 • Quantity - 6 Portions

Ingredients

2 Tablespoons of Butter
6 Cups of Cooked Chicken, scalloped
4 Cups of Creole Sauce, Formula No. 902

Procedure

Heat butter in pan, add chicken, simmer a few minutes) add hot Creole sauce. Simmer for five (5) minutes. Serve with Rice Pilaf.

Chicken Croquettes

Ingredients

1/2 Cup of Lard
2 Medium Onions, sliced fine
1/2 Teaspoon of Ground Thyme
1 Clove of Garlic, chopped fine
1 8 Oz. can of Mushrooms, diced 1/3 inch
6 Cups of Chicken, diced same, as Mushrooms
2 Pinches of ground Nutmeg
3 Cups of Cream Sauce - Formula No. 901
2 Yolks of Eggs
5 Tablespoons of Chives (if not available use
freshly chopped parsley)
Salt and Pepper
Worcestershire Sauce

Procedure

Heat lard in pan, add onion, thyme, garlic. Cook for two (2) minutes, add mushrooms) cook for two (2) more minutes. Add chicken, heat well together and sprinkle with nutmeg and add Cream Sauce, bring to a boil. Add diluted corn starch and cook for eight (8) minutes, then add beaten egg yolks, chives or parsley, after adding egg yolks take right off fire and blend thoroughly. Check seasoning, salt and pepper and worcestershire sauce.

This preparation should be made the day before to allow thorough cooling in cold box for breading purposes.

General Information As To

Cooking of Vegetables

To cook all green vegetables place in boiling salted water. When done but still firm, drain well and finish with a little butter and oleo mixed. Toss in shallow pan and season to taste,

In the case of Cauliflower, Broccoli and Asparagus, of course, melted butter and oleo should be sprinkled over it. They are especially nice with rich Cream sauce, or Hollandaise, Au Gratin and Polonaise Style.

For Cauliflower a stainless steel pot should be used and a little milk added to the water to keep it white. While cooking Cauliflower, Asparagus, Broccoli and Brussel Sprouts, be very cautious, not to let water boil too fast.

All vegetables should be kept firm as they are tastier and do not break up easily while handling.

General Information As To

Cooking of Starches - Spaghetti, Macaroni, Noodles

Starches should be cooked by placing them in boiling salted water.

If served as a side dish, drain when done, run a little hot water over it and add butter, salt and pepper.

If creamed or served with a brown sauce, just drain and proceed.

All starches should be cooked firm — not soft

For Rice we suggest Pilaf or Steamed Indian Style.

Varieties of Vegetables

Styles of Potatoes

Peas
String Beans
Lima Beans
Wax Beans
Spinach
Asparagus
Brussel Sprouts
Cauliflower
Cabbage - Red
Cabbage - White
Swiss Chard
Chinese Cabbage
Broccoli
Cucumber
Tomatoes
Corn
Carrots
Parsnips
Squash - Summer
Squash - Yellow
Squash - Hubbard
Turnips
Rutabagas
Beets
Celery
Mushroom
Green Peppers
Onions
Artichoke
Eggplant

French Fried
Home-Fried
O'Brien
Lyonnaise
Minute
Candied Yams and Sweets
Shoestring
Louisiana
Julienne
Hashed in Cream
Potatoes Chip
Hashed Brown
Mashed
Delmonico
Boiled
Duchesse
Baked
Baked Stuffed
Scalloped
Croquette
Potato Border
Hashed n Cream Au Gratin
Boiled with Butter and
Parsley
Sliced in Cream (Maitre
d'Hotel)
Cottage Fried or Baked
Oven Brown, Country Style
(Boulanger)

Notes

VEGETABLES & CEREALS

Peas-French Style

Ingredients

10 Pounds shelled peas - well washed
6 Strips of bacon, cut in 1/4 inch strips
1/2 Head Boston Lettuce - cut in coarse Julienne
21 Small White Onions - peeled
1 Teaspoon Salt
1 Pinch pepper
3 Tablespoons of Sugar
1 Teaspoon Chicken Base
Water to cover - about 3 cups
3 Tablespoons Flour
2 Tablespoons of Butter

Procedure

Render bacon slowly until half done - add onions and lettuce, let sinner for five (5) minutes. Add peas, salt, sugar, pepper, and chicken base, water, cover and cook slowly until peas are cooked. Mix butter and flour, add to peas and bring to a boil. Stir once when serving sprinkle with fresh chopped parsley.

(This recipe can be made with frozen peas and pre-cooked onions - in which case add onions to peas when almost cooled.)

Rice Pilaf

Formula No. 601 • 12 Servings
Ingredients

2-1/2 Cups of Rice
1/3 Cup of Lard
1 Medium Size onion - Chopped fine
2 Small Bay Leaves
4 Cups of Water
1 Tablespoon Chicken Base
Salt and Pepper to taste
2 Tablespoons of Butter

Procedure

Heat lard in pan, add onion and bay leaves, smother for a couple of minutes, do not allow to brown. Add washed rice and mix well; add water in which chicken base has been mixed and brought to a boil, bring to a boil; season to taste, cover with greased paper) cover pot and cook in hot oven for eighteen (18) minutes. Remove from pot into pan or Pyrex dish. Add the butter, mix well with roasting fork until rice is loosened. Cover with greased paper. Keep in warm place until served.

Stewed Tomatoes

Formula No. 602 • Quantity - 12 Garnish Portions
Ingredients

6 Medium Tomatoes
1 Small Chopped Onion
1 Tablespoon Oleo or Butter
1/2 Teaspoon Salt
1 Teaspoon Sugar
1 Pinch Ground Pepper

Procedure

Peel tomatoes, cut in half, Squeeze out seeds. Cut in large pieces, heat oleo or butter in pan, add onion, cook slowly but do not allow to brown. Add tomatoes, sugar, salt and pepper, simmer for three (3) minutes.

Serve as garnish as directed.

Candied Yams

Formula No. 603

Ingredients

Yams
Maple Syrup or Pancake Syrup
Oleo

Procedure

Boil yams in salt water until done, drain and let cool, peel, slice in slices 1/2 inch pieces, arrange in buttered baking dish, pour maple or pancake syrup over yams cook in hot oven, allowing same to brown slightly, while in oven baste from time to time.

Stewed Celery In Cream

Formula No. 604

Ingredients

Stalks of Celery
Juice of one lemon
Salt and pepper
Cream Sauce, Formula No. 901
Butter
Pinch grated nutmeg

Procedure

Trim celery stalks, scrape outside leaves with economy scraper, cut in 1/2 Inch pieces) wash thoroughly, plunge in boiling water to which salt and lemon juice have been added. Cook until done, drain and plunge in cold water. Put butter in pan, add celery, season to taste, heat slowly, add Cream Sauce, add Grated Nutmeg.

Braised Red Cabbage

Formula No. 605 • Quantity - 15 Garnitures

Ingredients

2 Tablespoons of Lard
1 Read Red Cabbage, sliced (3 lbs)
2 Medium onions, sliced
2 Bayleaves
1 Clove of Garlic
1/2 Cup of Apple Sauce
1 Cup Of Vinegar
2 Tablespoons of Sugar
Salt and Pepper

Procedure

Heat lard and add onions, bayleaves and garlic. Allow to brown very lightly, then add shredded Red Cabbage, mixing very well. Then add vinegar, apple sauce, sugar, salt and pepper. Cover with well fitting, greased paper. Simmer for a few minutes and finish in oven until thoroughly done. Check seasoning.

Carrots Vichy

Formula No. 606 • Quantity - 5 Garnitures

Ingredients

1/2 Gallon sliced carrots (4 lbs)
2 Teaspoons salt
1/2 Teaspoon pepper
2 Tablespoons sugar
2 Tablespoons butter
1 Teaspoon chicken base
1 Tablespoon freshly chopped parsley
Water to cover

Procedure

Put carrots, salt, pepper, sugar, butter, chicken base, and water in pan. Boil until carrots are done. Liquid should be almost evaporated. When serving sprinkle with chopped parsley.

Potato Pancake

Ingredients

6 Medium size raw Potatoes, peeled
2 Medium size Onions, chopped fine
2 Tablespoons of freshly chopped Parsley
2 Teaspoons of Salt
1/2 Teaspoon of ground Nutmeg
1 Teaspoon of ground Pepper
2 Whole Eggs
2 Cups of Flour
1/2 Cup of Milk
2 Teaspoons of Baking Powder

Procedure

Grind potatoes through grinder using large screen, put in bowl add onions, parsley, salt, nutmeg, pepper, mix well, add flour, blend well, add eggs, slightly beaten, add milk slowly, work until mixture is smooth, add baking powder.

Cook in a heated shallow pan in small quantity of lard, using basting spoon half filled and cook both sides until golden brown. Be sure pancake is cooked through.

Duchess Potatoes

Formula No. 608 • Quantity - 12 Portions

Ingredients

8 Medium Potatoes (or- 2-1/2 lbs.)
2 Tablespoons of Butter
2 Egg Yolks
Salt and Pepper

Procedure

Boil potatoes in salt water, when done drain out water and pass thru ricer. Add butter, salt and pepper. Blend well together and add yolks of eggs, set back on fire, stir well with wooden spoon for a few minutes, to allow eggs to cook. Be careful that potatoes do not burn on bottom of pot.

For Potato Border and Duchesse Potatoes use freshly made, for Croquette Potatoes,should be made day before and set in cold box overnight. Shaped, breaded and fried in deep fat to a golden brown.

Use No. 10 scoops for Duchesse and Croquette - one (1) per portion.

Buttered Beets
(Using whole canned beets)

Formula No. 609

Slice beets, nice and fine. Heat with just a little juice on bottom of pot.

Season with salt, pepper, sugar and a little Oleo. Simmer for a few minutes with cover on pot. When serving, use perforated basting spoon.

Stuffed Duchesse Potatoes

Formula No. 610 • Quantity - 12 Portions

Ingredients

8 Medium sized Potatoes
2 Tablespoons of Butter
2 Egg Yolks
Salt and Pepper
1/2 Cup of Onion, chopped fine
1/2 Cup of Ham, chopped fine
2 Tablespoons of freshly chopped parsley

Procedure

Boil potatoes in salt water, when done, drain and put through ricer; return to pot, add butter, salt and pepper; blend well with wooden spoon, add egg yolks and return to fire and cook while stirring, for two (2) minutes. Saute onions and ham until done, do not allow to brown, add to potatoes, blend well and add parsley. Place in buttered baking pan forming same round balls using No. 10 scoop. Sprinkle lightly with paprika and melted butter. Bake in hot oven until golden brown.

SALADS

Plain Cole Slaw

Formula No. 703 • Quantity - 18-20 Servings

Ingredients

1 Medium head cabbage
1 Medium onion, chopped fine
2 Tablespoons parsley chopped
2/3 Cups Mayonnaise
1 Oz. Vinegar
Salt and Pepper

Procedure

Cabbage head cut in 4, core cut out and shredded very fine; blended well with onions, parsley, mayonnaise, vinegar, and seasoned to taste served on a salad plate over a nice leaf of lettuce.

Chef's Salad Bowl

Formula No. 710 • Quantity - 1 Portion a la carte

Ingredients

Lettuce, Escarole or Chickory, Watercress
Just enough of each to make a handful or a bowlful
Ham
Tongue
Chicken
Tomato

Procedure

Shred lettuce, escarole, chickory and watercress and fill bowl. Cut Ham, Tongue and Chicken in Julienne one (1) inch long. Set in three (3) individual bunches on top of the Shredded Salad, separating each bunch with a small wedge of tomato. Place a bouquet of watercress on top center.

Desired dressing in goose neck.

Serve in individual salad bowl. If no salad bowl is available, use a cereal bowl.

Waldorf Salad

Ingredients

6 Celery, cleaned and diced, about 3 cups
18 Lettuce leaves
Apples, peeled, cored and diced, or 2 lbs.
3/4 Cups Mayonnaise
Salt and Pepper
2 oz. Vinegar
18 Teaspoons Walnuts, chopped

Procedure

Apples and Celery blended together with Mayonnaise, Vinegar, Salt and Pepper.

To serve, place one (1) leaf of lettuce, salt and pepper, and one (1) No. 10 scoop of salad in center of plate. One-half (1/2) teaspoon of Mayonnaise on top of salad. Sprinkle with Walnuts.

Pickled Beets

Ingredients

3 #2 Cans of Shoestring Beets
2 Medium Onions, sliced very fine
1/2 Juice of Beets
1 Cup Vinegar
3 Bayleaves
1 Small garlic clove, chopped very fine
2 Tablespoons sugar
Salt and Pepper
2 Tablespoons freshly chopped Parsley

Procedure

All ingredients well blend together and allowed to stand for a few hours at least.

Chicken Salad

Formula No. 713 • Quantity - 1 Portion a la carte

Ingredients

1 nice leaf of lettuce
1/3 cup celery, diced
2/3 cup of cooked chicken, diced
2 Wedges tomatoes
2 quarters of hard boiled eggs

Procedure

Place lettuce leaf on plate. Celery in center, chicken over celery. 1 wedge of tomatoes on opposite sides and quarter of egg on other sides.
Dressing in goose neck.

Lobster Salad

Formula No. 714 • Quantity 1 portion a la carte

Ingredients

1 nice leaf of lettuce
1/3 cup celery, diced
2/3 cup of cooked lobster
2 wedges tomatoes
2 quarters of hard boiled egg

Procedure

Place lettuce leaf on plate. Celery in center, lobster over celery. 1 wedge of tomato on opposite sides and quarter of egg on other sides.
Dressing in gooseneck.

Shrimp Salad

Formula No. 715 • Quantity -1 Portion a la carte

Ingredients

1 nice leaf of lettuce
1/3 cup celery, diced
2/3 cup of cooked shrimp, diced
2 wedges tomatoes
2 quarters of hard boiled egg

Procedure

Place lettuce leaf on plate, celery in center, shrimp over celery. 1 wedge of tomato on opposite sides and quarter of egg on other sides.

Dressing in gooseneck.

Cole Slaw - Mexican Style

Formula No. 716 • Quantity -12-24 Garnishing

Ingredients

1 Medium head white cabbage
2 Small green pepper (cut lengthwise, etc.)
1 Medium onion, chopped fine
40-48 strips pimento
2 Tablespoons parsley, chopped
2/3 Cup mayonnaise
Salt and Pepper

Procedure

Cabbage head cut in 4, core cut out and shredded very fine. Green pepper cut in 4, seeds removed and shredded very fine. Cabbage and pepper blended together with mayonnaise vinegar, salt and pepper to taste, chopped onion and chopped parsley.

In serving, place leaf of lettuce on salad plate, one (1) serving of cole slaw in center of lettuce.

Cole slaw to be topped with two (2) strips of pimento.

Shredded Lettuce and Asparagus Tip Salad

Formula No. 717 • Quantity -12

Ingredients

1 Head white lettuce
24 strips pimento
36 or 48 Asparagus tips - canned (according to size)

Procedure

Lettuce to be cut in four (4) and shredded very fine. Small amount of shredded lettuce to be placed on salad plate, just enough to cover bottom well. Four (4)s, all asparagus tips over lettuce, topped with two (2) strips of pimento.

Dressing in gooseneck.

Caution: In case of a long asparagus tip stem, use three (3) asparagus cut in half, placing stems over lettuce and tips over the stem. Top with two (2) strips of pimento.

Chiffonade Salad

Formula No. 718 • Quantity -18-20

Ingredients

1 Head lettuce
1 Head chickory
1 Bunch Watercress
18 Tomato Slices
2 Cups beets, chopped
4 Hard boiled eggs, chopped

Procedure

Salad and watercress cut up; well blended together. One (1) small handful placed on a salad plate, slice of tomato on top, chopped beets and eggs, freely sprinkled over all.

Dressing in gooseneck.

Lettuce, Celery and Cucumber Salad

Formula No. 719 • Quantity -10 Portions

Ingredients

10 Lettuce leaves
2 Cucumbers
2 Stems celery
1/2 Cup mayonnaise
1 Small onion, chopped fine
3 Teaspoons parsley, chopped fine
Salt and pepper
Few drops vinegar

Procedure

Peel cucumber, cut in half lengthwise and remove seeds with teaspoon, Then slice across real fine. Place in a bowl with a little salt to draw out water; and celery, scraped and washed. Then sliced across, real fine, imitating cucumber. Remove water out of cucumber and blend well with celery, adding chopped onion, mayonnaise, salt and pepper, vinegar, and chopped parsley.

In serving, place leaf of lettuce on salad plate, one (1) basting spoon of salad on leaf of lettuce.

Cole Slaw with Carrots, Celery and Cabbage

Formula No. 720 • Quantity - 24-28

Ingredients

1 Medium head cabbage, shredded finely
4 Stems celery, fine Julienne
2 Onions, fine
5-6 carrots, fine Julienne
2 Tablespoons Parsley, chopped
1 Cup mayonnaise
2 oz. Vinegar
Salt and Pepper

Procedure

Cabbage head cut in 4, core to be cut out, and quarters to be shredded very fine. Carrots and celery to be cut in Julienne, then all blended together with mayonnaise, vinegar, salt and pepper, chopped onions and parsley.

Serve one (1) basting spoon on leaf of lettuce on salad plate.

Fresh Fruit Salad

Formula No. 721 • Quantity -8 portions

Ingredients

1 Pear, 1 Apple or canned fruit
10 Grapefruit sections or 1 whole
10 Orange sections or 1 whole
1/2 Banana slice in 10
10 Grapes cut in halves
2 Maraschino cherries

Procedure

Pear and apple (or the canned fruit) peeled, cored and diced, placed in center of bowl lined with nice leaf of lettuce. Grapefruit section arranged in circle from center alternating with orange sections, slices of banana placed around outside at tip of orange sections and halves of grapes at tips of grapefruit section, maraschino cherry in top center.

Dressing in gooseneck.

Mixed Green Salad

Formula No. 722 • Quantity -24 portions

Ingredients

1 Head lettuce
1 Head chickory
1 Head escarole
1 Bunch Watercress
Dressing

Procedure

Cut up salad and watercress about 1" long, and blend well together.
Place one (1) small handful on salad plate.
Dressing in gooseneck

Fresh Fruit Cocktail

Formula No. 723 • Quantity -5 portions

Ingredients

1 Pear (or canned fruit)
1 Apple (or canned fruit)
10 Grapefruit sections or 1 whole
10 Orange sections or 1 whole
5 Maraschino cherries

Procedure

Pear and apple peeled, cored and diced, or canned fruits, set in cocktail glass. Grapefruit sections on opposite side, 2 orange sections in center and 1 maraschino cherry on top center.

Notes

SANDWICHES

Hot Turkey Sandwich

Formula No. 800

Ingredients

2 Slices toasted white bread, buttered
2 Tablespoons stuffing, Formula No. 909
1 Slice dark Turkey meat
2 Slices white Turkey meat
Family Gravy, Formula No. 910

Procedure

Place one slice of toasted bread on hot plate, spread with stuffing, put dark turkey meat, then white turkey meat, cut other slice of toast crosswise in triangle place on each side of the covered toast, cover with very hot family gravy.

Garnish with slice of tomato and slice of pickle on small leaf of lettuce.

Cold Turkey Sandwich - Chessie Style

Formula No. 801 • Quantity - 1 Portion

Ingredients

2 Slices white sandwich bread
2 Tablespoons turkey stuffing, Formula No. 923
1 Slice dark meat of turkey
2 Slices white meat of turkey
1 Leaf Lettuce
1 Slice Tomato
1 Piece Dill Pickle
1 Teaspoon Mayonnaise dressing

Procedure

Spread stuffing on white bread, place dark meat on stuffing, the white meat on top, put leaf of lettuce and slice of tomato, spread mayonnaise, cover with other slice of bread. Put slice of pickle on top of bread.

General Information As To-

Preparation of Clear Stocks

Use bones well washed and blanched if needed. Add onion, celery, carrots, bayleaves, thyme, cloves, garlic, trimming of vegetables are to be saved, used for this purpose. When boiling slow down fire and simmer only, keeping on the fire for a few hours skimming right along; when flavor is well cooked out of bones, strain and cook.

General Information As To-

Preparation of Brown Stock

Brown up bones in oven with vegetables and herbs, then follow same operation as clear stock. Add trimming of tomatoes left-overs of any kind of tomato sauce or brown gravies. You should use this stock to finish all Roast Gravies.

Notes

DRESSINGS & SAUCES

The George Washington

Cocktail Sauce

Formula No. 900 • Quantity - 1 Quart

Ingredients

1-3/4 Cups Chili Sauce
1-3/4 Cups Catsup
1/2 Cup Horse Radish
1/4 Cup Chopped Chow Chow
1 Teaspoon Worcestershire Sauce

Procedure

Mix all above ingredients add salt and pepper to taste.

Cream Sauce

Formula No. 901 • Quantity- 1 Quart

Ingredients

1 Quart of milk
1/2 Cup of lard
1/2 Stalk of celery, sliced fine
1 Small onion, sliced fine
1 Bayleaf
5 Tablespoons of flour
Season to taste

Procedure

(Total cooking time 25 minutes)

Heat lard in pan; add onion and celery, bayleaf, simmer without allowing same to color. Add flour and mix well. Cook very slowly for 4 or 5 Minutes. Add the milk which has been brought to a boil. Stir well until same comes to a boil. Cook for 15 minutes more and then strain through fine strainer without pressure. Season to taste.

Creole Sauce

Ingredients

1/2 Cup of lard
2 Medium sized onions, sliced
2 Green peppers, cored, with seeds taken out; and sliced
2 Cups of sliced mushrooms
2 Bayleaves
1 Pinch of ground thyme
2 Cloves of garlic crushed and chopped
1 No. 2-1/2 can of whole tomatoes
1 Cup of water
1/2 Teaspoon of Chicken Base
1 Tablespoon of corn starch
Salt and pepper to taste

Procedure

(Total cooking time 30 minutes)

Heat lard in pan and add onions, peppers and mushrooms, and simmer for five minutes.

Add tomato, garlic, thyme and bayleaves and water, and base, simmer for 20 minutes more. Dilute cornstarch in small quantity of cold water, bring to a boil, and use as wanted.

P.S. If used for Spanish Omelet; increase quantity of cornstarch to two tablespoons.

Hollandaise Sauce

Formula No. 903 • Quantity - 20 Servings

Ingredients

1 Pound Butter
5 Egg Yolks
1/2 Teaspoon Salt
Juice of one (1) Lemon
Dash of Cayenne Pepper

Procedure

Melt butter slowly, allow to stand so that water settles on bottom.

Put yolks in heavy round bottom pot and add teaspoon of warm water. Submerge bottom of pan in hot water, beat continually until eggs have creamy consistency (take care not to let eggs scramble), Remove from hot water, add melted butter slowly (do not allow bottom of pan, namely water, residue, to drop in the mixture.) This mixture should have the consistency of mayonnaise dressing. Add lemon juice, salt and cayenne pepper. Transfer to a stainless steel bainmarie. Keep in warn place.

Lemon Butter
(For use on broiled items)

Formula No. 904

Ingredients

1/4 Pound Butter
Juice of 1/2 lemon
1 Teaspoon freshly chopped parsley
Dash Cayenne Pepper

Procedure

Blend together in small bowl until thoroughly mixed.

Polonaise Dressing

Formula No. 905 • Quantity -18 Dressings

Ingredients

2 Cups of fresh white breadcrumbs
2 Chopped hard boiled eggs
2 Tablespoons of freshly chopped parsley
1/2 Cup of Lard or Butter
Salt and Pepper

Procedure

Heat lard or butter, add bread crumbs, cook until light brown, remove from fire, add chopped eggs and parsley, salt and pepper, use as directed in formulas.

Tomato Sauce

Formula No. 906 • Quantity - 1/2 Gallon

Ingredients

1/2 Cup of Lard or 1 cup of Ham or Pork trimmings
1 Medium sized Onion, cut in small squares
1 Medium sized Carrot, cut in small squares
2 Outside stalks of Celery, cut in small squares
2 Bayleaves
1 Pinch of ground Thyme
2 Cloves of Garlic, crushed
1 Quart of Tomato Puree
2 Quarts of Water
2 Tablespoons of Chicken Base
3 Tablespoons of Corn Starch
1 Tablespoon of Sugar
Salt and Pepper
(Cooking time fifty (50) minutes)

Procedure

Heat lard or trimmings in pan and add onion, carrot, celery. Simmer for ten (10) minutes. Then add garlic, tomato, bayleaf, thyme, stock and sugar; simmer for thirty-five (35) minutes. Season to taste. Add corn starch diluted in small quantity of cold water, bring to a boil, strain through fine Strainer.

This base can be used for Creme of Tomato in an emergency by adding equal quantity of Cream Sauce to Tomato Sauce. Add small quantity of fresh butter.

Sour Cream Gravy

Formula No. 907 • Quantity - 1 Quart

Ingredients

1 Tablespoon Oleo
1/2 Cup Ham Trimmings, cut small
1/2 Cup Vinegar
1/2 Cup Sliced Onions
4 Cups Creme Sauce - Formula No. 901
1/2 Cup Light Cream
1 Pinch Nutmeg
Salt and Pepper to taste

Procedure

Heat oleo in pan, add ham, cook until ham is golden brown, add onions let cook until light brown. Add vinegar and let simmer for five (5) minutes, add cream, sauce, boil for ten (10) minutes, strain, add cream, season to taste.

Italian Tomato Sauce

Formula No. 908 • Quantity - 1/2 Gallon

Ingredients

1/2 Cup Lard
2 Medium sized onions, sliced
1 Bayleaf
1 Pinch thyme
2 Basil leaves (if available)
2 Clove garlic, chopped
2 No. 2-1/2 Cans whole tomatoes
1 Cup tomato puree
2 Cups of water
1 Teaspoon chicken base
1 Tablespoon corn starch
2 Tablespoons freshly chopped Parsley

Procedure

Heat lard in pan, add onion, bayleaf, thyme, basil leaves, garlic, simmer a few minutes, add tomatoes, tomato puree, water, chicken base, cook slowly for forty (40) minutes, take out bayleaf, add corn starch diluted in small quantity of cold water, bring to a boil. Season to taste, add parsley. Do not strain.

Bread Stuffing

Formula No. 909 • Quantity - 35 Garnishings

Ingredients

2 Tablespoons of lard
2 Medium sized Onions, chopped
1-1/2 Cups of Ham trimmings, chopped fine
1 Two (2) Pound loaf of White Bread or equal amount of stale
white bread trimmings
3 Cups of milk
1 Teaspoon of Salt
2 Pinches of Ground Black Pepper
1/2 Teaspoon of ground Sage
2 Pinches ground Thyme
2 Whole Eggs
1/2 Cup of freshly chopped Parsley
1 Cup of Family Gravy, Formula No. 910

Procedure

Soak bread in three cups of milk, if too dry add a little more milk. Heat lard in skillet, add onions and ham. Cook with out allowing to color for five (5) minutes. Put in bowl, add ground bread, pepper, salt, thyme, sage, eggs. Mix well with wooden spoon. Put in greased baking pan. Cover with greased paper. Put in oven until heated through, about fifteen (15) minutes. When done, add one cup of Family Gravy and parsley. Mix well, keep hot or cool off for cold sandwich.

Family Gravy

Formula 910 • Quantity - 1 Quart

Ingredients

2 Tablespoons of lard
1 Small Onion, diced fine
1 Small Carrot, diced fine
1/2 Stem of Celery, diced fine
1 Bayleaf
3 Cups of hot water
1 Tablespoon of Chicken Base
1 Cup Whole Canned Tomatoes
1 Teaspoon of Corn Starch
Few dashes of Maggi and Kitchen Bouquet
Salt and Pepper to taste

Procedure

Heat lard in pan, add onion, carrot, celery, bayleaf, cook until golden brown. Add tomato, hot water, chicken base; cook for twenty (20) minutes, add corn starch diluted in a little cold water, bring to a boil. Strain through fine chinese Strainer. Season to taste, add Maggi and Kitchen Bouquet.

Curry Sauce

Formula No. 911 • Quantity - 1 Gallon

Ingredients

1/2 Cup of Lard
3 Medium sized onions, chopped fine
1 Cup of Flour
3 Tablespoons Curry Powder
3-1/2 Quarts of hot water
3 Tablespoon of Chicken Base
1 Cup tomato puree
2 oz. Shredded Coconut
1 Cup of Apple Sauce
1 Cup Chutney, chopped
Salt and Pepper to taste

Procedure

Heat lard in pan, add onions, simmer slowly without browning for five (5) minutes add curry powder, blend well, add flour, blend well, cook for two (2) minutes. Add hot water, tomato puree, chicken base. Cook slowly for twenty (20) minutes, add apple sauce, coconut, cook for ten (10) minutes, add chutney, season with salt and pepper to taste. Do not strain.

Raisin Sauce

Formula No. 912 • Quantity - 1 Quart

Ingredients

1 Quart Family Gravy - Formula No. 910
1 Cup Raisins, soaked in boiling water
1/2 Cup Currant Jelly
2 Tablespoons of Sugar
1 Tablespoon of Vinegar
1 Pinch of Ground Cloves

Procedure

Put vinegar and sugar in pan, let cook until vinegar is almost evaporated, add currant jelly, and Family Gravy. Let cook for five (5) minutes, add raisins, ground cloves, let cook slowly for five (5) minutes. P.S. This sauce should have consistency of a syrup and can be thickened if desired, by adding a little corn starch diluted in cold water.

Pineapple Sauce

Formula No. 913 • Quantity - 1 Quart

Ingredients

3 Cups of Family Gravy - Formula No. 910
1 Cup of Pineapple Juice
1 Cup Sliced Pineapple, cut in small strips
2 Tablespoons of Sugar
1 Tablespoon of Vinegar
1 Pinch of Ground Cloves
1 Bayleaf

Procedure

Put vinegar and sugar in pan, boil until vinegar is almost evaporated, add pineapple juice, ground cloves, bayleaf, family gravy, cook for ten (10) minutes, remove bayleaf. Add pineapple strips, cook for five (5) minutes.

P.S. This sauce should have consistency of a syrup and can be thickened if desired; by adding a little corn starch diluted in cold water.

Cider Sauce

Formula No. 914 • Quantity - 1 Quart

Ingredients

2 Cups of Family Gravy - Formula No. 910
2 Cups of Cider Preferably Cider in which ham has baked
2 Tablespoons of Sugar
1 Tablespoon of Vinegar
1 Pinch of Ground Cloves
1 Bayleaf

Procedure

Put vinegar and sugar in pan, cook until vinegar is almost evaporated, add family gravy, cider, ground clove, bayleaf. Cook for ten (10) minutes, remove bayleaf.

P.S. This sauce should have consistency of syrup and can be thickened if desired; by adding a little corn starch diluted in cold water.

Orange Sauce

Formula No. 915 • Quantity 1 Quart

Ingredients

1 Quart of Family Gravy - Formula No. 910
3/4 Cup of Orange Marmalade
2 Tablespoons of Sugar
1 Tablespoons of Vinegar
1 Pinch of Ground Clove
1 Bayleaf

Procedure

Put vinegar and sugar in pan, cook until vinegar has evaporated, add Family Gravy, ground clove, bayleaf, cook for five (5) minutes, remove bayleaf, add orange marmalade, cook for five (5) minutes.

P.S. This sauce should have consistency of syrup and can be thickened if desired; by adding a little corn starch diluted in cold water.

Fruit Sauce

Formula No. 916 • Quantity 1 Quart

Ingredients

3 Cups of Family Gravy, Formula No. 910
1 Cup Pineapple Juice
1/3 Cup Raisins, soaked in boiling water
1/3 Cup Pineapple, cut in small strips
1/2 Cup of raw apple, peeled and cut in small strips
2 Tablespoons of Currant Jelly
2 Tablespoons of Sugar
1 Tablespoon of Vinegar
1 Pinch of Ground Clove
1 Bayleaf

Procedure

Put vinegar and sugar in pan, cook until vinegar is evaporated, add family gravy, pineapple juice, ground clove, bayleaf, bring to a boil, add apples, cook for ten (10) minutes, remove bayleaf, add pineapple, raisins, currant jelly. Cook for five (5) minutes.

P.S. This sauce should have consistency of syrup and can be thickened if desired; by adding a little corn starch diluted in cold water.

Tartare Sauce

Formula No. 917 • Quantity - 1 Quart

Ingredients

1 Quart of Mayonnaise
1 Cup Onions, chopped very fine
4 Dill Pickles, chopped very fine
4 Tablespoons of Capers, chopped very fine
2 Tablespoons of freshly chopped Parsley
1 Pinch of ground Pepper
Few dashes of Worcestershire Sauce

Procedure

Put chopped onion, dill pickles, capers in cloth, press out all moisture, add mayonnaise, parsley, pepper and worcestershire sauce, blend well. Check seasoning.

Russian Dressing

Formula No. 918 • Quantity - Quart

Ingredients

2-1/2 Cups of Mayonnaise
1 Cup Chili Sauce
1/2 Cup Onion, finely chopped
3 Hard Boiled Eggs, chopped
3 Tablespoons Chives or Parsley
Few dashes of Worcestershire Sauce

Procedure

Blend all above ingredients properly.

1000 Island Dressing

Formula No. 919 • Quantity - 1 Quart

Ingredients

3 Cups of Russian Dressing - Formula No. 918
1 Cup of Beets, chopped very fine
2 Cups of Whipped Cream

Procedure

Blend all above ingredients properly.

Dessert Fruit Sauce

Formula No. 920 • Quantity - 1 Gallon (50 Servings)

Ingredients

6 Cups of Fruit Cocktail
1 Cup of Raisins
2 Quarts of Nectarine or Apricot Juice
2 Cups of Water
1/2 Cup of Sugar
1/2 Teaspoon of Vanilla Extract
8 Drops of Lemon Extract
3 Tablespoons of Corn Starch

Procedure

Mix fruit cocktail, apricot or nectarine juice, raisins (washed in cold water), sugar, vanilla and lemon extract, bring to a boil, for two (2) minutes. Add corn starch, diluted in a small quantity of cold water; bring to a boil, let cool and serve as directed.

Nectarine Sauce

Formula No. 921 • Quantity - 1 Quart

Ingredients

4 Cups of Apricot Juice
2 Tablespoons of Sugar
1 Teaspoon of Cornstarch
(diluted in small amount of cold water)
A few drops of Vanilla flavor

Procedure

Boil Apricot juice, add sugar, vanilla flavor and cornstarch, strain. Cool before serving.

Bearnaise Sauce

Formula No. 922 • Quantity - 1 Quart

Ingredients

1 Quart of Hollandaise Sauce - Formula No. 903
1/2 Cup of Tarragon Vinegar
1/4 Teaspoon whole pepper, crushed
1-1/2 Tablespoons of Chopped parsley
1/2 Teaspoon of chopped fresh Tarragon (If available)
Few drops of Maggi

Procedure

Put vinegar and pepper in pot, boil until the vinegar is almost evaporated. Strain and add one quart of Hollandaise Sauce, Formula No. 905. Check seasoning and add chopped parsley, tarragon, Maggi and stir well.

Stuffing Spread For Cold Turkey or Chicken Sandwich

Formula No. 923 • Quantity- 1 Quart

Ingredients

2 Cups of Bread Stuffing, Formula No. 909
2 Cups of Mayonnaise

Procedure

Using half and half bread stuffing, mayonnaise, well blended together after stuffing is cold. Check seasoning.

Cheese Cream Sauce
(Mornay Sauce)

Formula No. 924 • Quantity - 1 Quart

Ingredients

1/2 Cup of Lard
1/2 Stalk of Celery, sliced fine
1 Small Onion, sliced fine
1 Bayleaf
5 Tablespoons of Flour
1 Quart of Milk
4 Tablespoons (Heaping) of grated Parmesan Cheese
Season to taste

Procedure

Heat lard in pot, add onions, celery, bayleaf, simmer without browning up. Add flour blend well, cook slowly for 4 or 5 minutes. Add the milk which has been brought to a boil. Stir well until same comes to a boil, add cheese. Cook for five (5) more minutes, when ready strain through fine strainer without pressure. Season to taste.

Au Gratin

To make a dish, whether vegetable or meat Au Gratin: cover it with cheese cream sauce - Formula No. 924, sprinkling Parmesan grated cheese over it and brown up in a very hot oven or under a broiler, until golden brown.

Meat Sauce Italian Style

Formula 926 • Quantity - 1 Quart

Ingredients

1-1/2 Cup of Lard
2 Cups of Ground Beef (1 lb.)
2 Medium Onions, sliced
1 Bayleaf
1 Pinch of Thyme
2 Basil Leaves (If available)
2 Cloves of Garlic, chopped fine
2 #2-1/2 Cans of Whole Tomatoes (cut up)
1 Cup of Tomato Puree
2 Cups of Water
1 Teaspoon of Chicken Base
1 Tablespoon of Corn Starch
2 Tablespoons of freshly chopped Parsley

Procedure

Heat lard in sauce pan, add meat and brown up a little, then add onions, bayleaf, thyme, basil leaves, garlic. Cook together for a few minutes without browning up, add tomatoes, tomato puree, water, chicken base. Cook slowly for forty (40) minutes, take out bayleaf, add diluted corn starch simmer town (2) minutes more, check seasoning and add parsley. Do not strain.

Horseradish Sauce

Formula No. 927 • Quantity - 1 Quart

Ingredients

1 Quart of Cream Sauce - Formula No. 901
1 Cup of Horseradish, grated freshly or bottled
Few dashes of Worcestershire Sauce
Salt and Pepper

Procedure

Bring Cream Sauce to a boil, add horseradish and Worcestershire sauce. Season to taste.

Egg Sauce

Formula No. 928 • Quantity - 1 Quart

Ingredients

1 Quart of Cream Sauce - Formula No. 901
3 Hard Boiled Eggs, not chopped too fine
1 Teaspoon of prepared custard
Few dashes of Worcestershire Sauce
Salt and Pepper

Procedure

Bring Cream Sauce to a boil, add chopped eggs, mustard and Worcestershire sauce. Season to taste.

Italian Mushroom Sauce

Formula No. 929 • Quantity - 2 Quarts

Ingredients

2 Tablespoons of Butter
1 Pint of fresh sliced mushrooms
2 Quarts of Italian Tomato Sauce Formula No. 908

Procedure

Heat butter in pan, add mushrooms and saute until done; add Italian Tomato Sauce bring to a boil. Cook two (2) Minutes. Check seasoning.

Red Wine Mushroom Sauce

Formula No. 930 • Quantity - 1 Quart

Ingredients

2 Tablespoons of Butter
1/2 Pint of fresh sliced Mushrooms
4 Oz. of Red Wine
1 Quart of Family Gravy - Formula No. 910

Procedure

Heat butter in pan, add mushrooms and saute about two (2) minutes, add wine, simmer for two (2) minutes; add Family Gravy, boil for two (2) minutes. Check seasoning.

Apple and Prune Stuffing

Formula No. 931 • Quantity - 25 to 30 Garnishings

Ingredients

2 Pounds of Prunes
3 Pounds of Cooking Apples
1/2 Cup of Sugar
1 Pinch of ground cloves
1/4 Teaspoon of ground Cinnamon
Juice of two Lemons

Procedure

Soak prunes over night. Cook in water used for soaking prunes until done, remove pits from prunes.

Peel apples, cut in quarters and remove core. Slice in thick slices, mix with prunes and add sugar, ground cloves, ground cinnamon and lemon juice; blend well and bake in small baking pan for twenty (20) minutes.

Mustard Cream Sauce

Formula No. 932 • Quantity -1 Quart

Ingredients

1 Quart of Cream Sauce - Formula No. 901
2 Level Tablespoons of English Mustard
Few dashes of Worcestershire Sauce

Procedure

Dilute mustard in small quantity of cold water, add to boiling Cream Sauce, cook for two (2) minutes, add worcestershire sauce. Check Seasoning.

Notes

DESSERTS

THE
Fast Flying F.F.V. Virginian

Bread and Butter Pudding

Formula No. 1001 • Quantity - 8 to 10 Portions

Ingredients

1 Quart of Milk
1 Cup of granulated Sugar
6 Eggs
8 Slices of Sandwich Bread, 1/4 inch thick, well buttered,
trimmed and cut in 4 so it will result in 4 triangles
3/4 Cup of Seeded Raisins
1/4 Cup of Currants
1 Demi Tasse spoon of Vanilla Extract or 1/4 Vanilla Bean, split

Procedure

(Cooking time thirty-five minutes)

Put 1/2 the quantity of raisins and currants in the bottom of an oblong pyrex utility dish, capacity about 2-3/4 quarts. Arrange sliced, buttered bread in systematic rows, the pointed end up, to cover the entire bottom of dish. Put milk in a pan and bring to a boil. Mix raw eggs and sugar in a bowl until creamy. Pour boiling milk over eggs and sugar mixture, strain and add vanilla extract (if vanilla bean is used put in milk when bring same to a boil.) Skim off all foam. Pour above strained mixture over bread with a ladle, taking care not to disturb the bread. Be sure that all bread has been covered with the mixture. Sprinkle balance of raisins and currants over mixture. Put the dish in a shallow pan with hot water and cook, in oven as you would a custard. Average temperature 375 degrees. Increase heat the last five (5) minutes to give color to top of pudding. Serve hot or cold, with cream, if desired.

Coupe Chessie

Formula No. 1002 • Quantity - 1 Portion

Ingredients

1 Small cut sponge cake
1 Scoop vanilla ice cream (or half brick)
1 Tablespoon frozen strawberries
1 Teaspoon Melba Sauce

Procedure

Place sponge cake in cold dessert dish, place ice cream on top, add strawberries, and cover top with Melba Sauce.

Custard Desserts

Formula No. 1003 • Quantity - 7 Portions

Ingredients

1 Quart of Milk
6 Whole Eggs
1/2 Teaspoon of flavoring to taste (Vanilla, Orange or Lemon)

Procedure

Mix eggs, sugar and milk, beat well, add desired flavor, pour into individual custard or pyrex pan which has been buttered and sugared, put same in pan with hot water, cook in oven until firm, do not allow water to boil, let cool. Serve cold, turning over in dish, under fruit or sauce covering, or plain.

Fresh Fruit Jello

Formula - No. 1004 • Quantity - 14 Portions

Ingredients

2 Sliced Bananas
2 Raw apples, peeled, quartered and sliced
2 Fresh peaches (or pears, according to season)
peeled, quartered, and sliced.
2 Oranges, peeled, sectioned and each section cut in half
1 Quart of Water
1 Cup of Strawberry or Cherry Jello

Procedure

Put fruit in pan mixing well so that all types are properly distributed. Heat one cup of water, dissolve Jello, add to the balance of water three (3) cups which should be cold; mix well. let set in refrigerator.

Lemon Filling

Formula - No. 1005 • Quantity - 6-10" Pies

Ingredients

10-1/2 Cups of Water
9 Cups of Sugar
5 Oz. of Butter
2-1/2 Cups of Corn Starch
3 Cups of Lemon Juice
1/2 Cup of grated Lemon rind
24 Egg Yolks
1 Cup of Cold Milk

Procedure

Put water, sugar and butter in pan, bring to a boil, dilute corn starch in 1/2 cup of cold water and add to mixture.

Add lemon juice. Cook for eight (8) minutes Beat egg yolks well with cold milk and add to mixture. Bring to a boil, cook for two (2) minutes.

Old Fashioned Strawberry Shortcake

Formula No. 1006 • Quantity - 1 Portion

Ingredients

1 Baking powder biscuit, Formula No. 1207
1 Serving spoon frozen (or fresh crushed) Strawberries
1 Tablespoon whipped cream, sugared

Procedure

Cut baking powder biscuit in two, toast, place one-half in dessert dish, pour on strawberries, cover with other half of biscuit - put whipped cream on top.

Pastry Filling Cream

Formula No. 1007 • Quantity - 15 fillings

Ingredients

1 Quart Milk
12 Yolks of Eggs
1 Cup Flour
2 Cups Sugar
1/4 Teaspoon vanilla extract

Procedure

Mix flour and sugar together, blend well, add eggs, beat until well blended. Bring milk to a boil, pour over above mixture, stir well, put in pan, cook until it thickens, pour in bowl, let cool, stirring from time to time.

Deep Dish Apple Pie

Formula No. 1008 • Quantity - 24 Portions

Ingredients

20 Green Apples, large
1/2 Teaspoon of Ground Cinnamon
3/4 Cup of Sugar
3 Cups of Water
1/2 Teaspoon of Ground Cloves
1 Teaspoon of grated Lemon rind
Pie Dough; Formula No. 1206, to cover

Procedure

Peel and core apples, cut in 8, put in pan, add cinnamon, sugar, water, cloves, grated lemon rind; heat through, let cool, put in 16x11-1/2 inch stainless steel roast pan. Cover with pie dough rolled to thickness as for pie. Brush with raw beaten eggs mixed with cold water. Cook until pie crust is golden color and crisp. Serve in portions in fruit dish.

Pumpkin Pie

Formula No. 1009 • Quantity - 6 Pies

Ingredients

4 No. 2-1/2 Cans of Pumpkin
12 Eggs
1-1/2 Teaspoons of Ground Ginger
1 Teaspoon of Ground Cloves
2 Teaspoons 0f powdered Cinnamon
1/2 Cup melted Butter
4 Cups of Milk
3 Cups of Sugar
1/2 Cup of Molasses
Pie Dough, Formula No. 1206

Procedure

Add to Pumpkin - eggs slightly beaten, ginger, ground cloves, cinnamon, milk, sugar, molasses. Mix well and add melted butter. Fill pie plates lined with partly precooked pie dough. Cook in medium oven until done. Let cool and serve.

Canned Fruit Jello

Formula No. 1010 • Quantity - 14 Portions

Ingredients

1 No. 2-1/2 can of fruit cocktail
1 Raw, peeled, diced apple
2 Peeled and diced navel oranges
1 Cup of Jello - Strawberry or Cherry
1 Quart of Water

Procedure

Place fruit in shallow pan, dissolve Jello in one (1) cup of hot water. Mix with balance three (3) cups of cold water, blend well, pour over fruit. Place in refrigerator to set.

Coupe Hawaii

Formula No. 1011 • Quantity - 1 Portion

Ingredients

1 Ring of canned Pineapple
1 Scoop of Vanilla Ice Cream
1 Tablespoon of Frozen Strawberries

Procedure

Place ring of pineapple in cold fruit saucer; place ice cream on top and cover with frozen strawberries.

Rice Pudding

Formula No. 1012 • Quantity - 14 Portions

Ingredients

2 Quarts of Milk
1 Cup of Sugar
1/2 Teaspoon of Vanilla Flavor
6 Drops of Lemon Flavor
1 Cup of Rice
1 Tablespoon of Cinnamon powder
2 Tablespoons of Granulated Sugar

Procedure

Put milk in pot add sugar bring to a boil, add washed rice, cook slowly, stirring occasionally until done. Add flavors, (vanilla and lemon), pour in pyrex dish. Sprinkle with Cinnamon powder and granulated sugar mixed. Place in hot oven until done.

Pear Melba

Formula No. 1013 • Quantity - 1 Portion

Ingredients

1 Scoop of Vanilla Ice Cream
1/2 Canned Pear
1 Tablespoon of Melba Sauce

Procedure

Place Vanilla ice cream in very cold saucer, place pear on top, cover with melba sauce.

Peach Melba

Formula No. 1014 • Quantity - 1 Portion

Ingredients

1 Scoop of Vanilla Ice Cream
1/2 Canned Peach
1 Tablespoon of Melba Sauce

Procedure

Place Vanilla ice cream in very cold saucer, place peach on top, cover with melba sauce.

Mince Pie

Formula No. 1015 • Quantity - 6-10" Pies

Ingredients

6 Quarts of Mince Meat
6 Teaspoons of Corn Starch
Pie Dough, Formula No. 1206

Procedure

Blend Mince meat and corn starch well before filling pie crust. Proceed as usual, do not roll dough thin.
Serve Warm.

Meringue Topping

Formula No. 1016 • Quantity - 6-10" Pies

Ingredients

24 Egg Whites
3 Cups of Confectioners XXXX Sugar
Few dashes of Lemon Juice
1 Pinch of Salt

Procedure

Place white of eggs in a very clean bowl and add lemon juice and salt, beat well until firm. Add sugar and blend well. Top pie, smooth with spatula to a nice flat surface, sprinkle with a small amount of XXXX sugar. Bake in a very hot oven to a nice golden brown.

Sour Pitted Cherry Pie

Formula No. 1017 • Quantity - 6 - 10 inch Pies

Ingredients

12 No. 2-1/2 Cans of Sour Pitted Cherries
4 Bayleaves
10 Whole Cloves
3 Teaspoons powdered Cinnamon
6 Cups of Sugar
1 Cup of Corn Starch
1/2 Teaspoon Vanilla Flavor
Pie Dough - Formula No. 1206

Procedure

Drain juice off Cherries, place half of quantity of juice in sauce pan, add bay leaves, cloves, cinnamon, sugar, bring to a boil, add corn starch diluted in small quantity of cold cherry juice. Cook for two (2) minutes, add vanilla flavor. Strain through fine strainer and let cool.

Prebake pie bottom placing greased pie plate on top to prevent puffing. When partly cooked remove liner and fill with cherries, covering same with cherry sauce, allowing just enough juice to cover cherries; finish baking, let cool. When serving top each portion with tablespoon of whipped cream.

Apple Pie

Formula No. 1018 • Quantity - 6 - 10 inch Pies

Ingredients

30 Cooking Apples (about 10-1/2 pounds)
4-1/2 Cups of Sugar
3 Teaspoons ground Cinnamon
1/2 Cup of Lemon Juice
6 Tablespoons of Butter
Pie Dough - Formula No. 1206

Procedure

Peel apples, cut in quarters, core and slice (not too fine); put in bowl, add butter, sugar, cinnamon, lemon juice. Mix all well together, line pie plates with pie dough, fill with apples, prepare as above, very generously as apples will cook down. Cover with pie dough, brush with egg wash. Cook in medium oven for about fifty-five (55) minutes.

Notes

BEVERAGES

The Sportsman

Coffee

Coffee must be made over the bag, right in the Coffee Urn. The bag should be cleaned thoroughly, not staying in urn more than five (5) minutes after coffee is finished. When bag is washed it should be kept in cold water to prevent drying as drying and exposure causes it to become rancid, which gives the coffee a bitter and strong taste. As the bag starts to get dark brown it should be changed. Keep urn well cleaned and rinse every time you make fresh coffee.

For Iced Coffee make coffee stronger as it will be diluted by ice.

Tea

Formula No. 1102

Tea should be infused. Infusing means to be placed in boiling water, covered immediately and taken off fire. Let it stay covered for a little while, then remove tea bags. If tea is made from hot water urn, the water should be poured over bag boiling hot to give proper results.

For Iced Tea, tea should be made stronger as it will be diluted by ice.

Hot Cocoa

Formula No. 1103

Dilute Cocoa in very hot water and finish with boiling milk. For quantities, follow directions on package.

For Iced Cocoa, make stronger as it will be diluted by ice.

Hot Chocolate

Formula No. 1104

Shave Milk Sweetened or hard Baker's Chocolate, put in pan with small quantity of water, bring to a boil and stir until smooth. Add milk and heat to boiling point.

For Iced Chocolate, make stronger as the ice will dilute it.

Hot Chocolate prepared this way should be sweetened by the guest at the table.

Prepared Chocolate Powder can also be used by following the instructions on package.

Lemonade and Orangeade

Formula No. 1105

Lemonade and Orangeade should be made fresh, using the juice of the fruit, sugar and water. Do not make too sweet and be sure that it has a good fruit flavor.

Garnish with thin slices of the fruit and serve nice and cold.

Notes

CORN BREAD, MUFFINS, DOUGHS & CRUSTS

Corn Bread

Formula No. 1200 • Quantity - 8 Portions

Ingredients

1-1/2 Cup yellow corn meal
1-1/2 Cup flour
2 Teaspoons salt
1 Tablespoon sugar
4 Teaspoons baking powder
2 Whole Eggs
4 Tablespoons melted lard
1-1/2 Cup milk.

Procedure

Mix flour, corn meal, salt, sugar and baking powder, beat eggs and milk well, add to dry mixture) mix very well, add melted lard) mix until smooth, pour in baking pan, cook until golden brown.

Corn Fritters

Formula No. 1201 • Quantity - 24 Fritters

Ingredients

20 Ounce can of corn, drained
2 Cups flour
3 Teaspoons salt
4 Tablespoons sugar
4 Teaspoons baking powder
2/3 Cup of Milk
2 Whole Eggs

Procedure

Mix flour, salt, sugar, baking powder, add eggs and milk - mix until smooth, add corn, pour in hot shortening in shallow pan using basting spoon 2/3 full for each fritter, cook until golden brown on each side. When done, put on clean paper to draw off excess shortening. Serve hot.

Corn Muffins

Formula No. 1202 • Quantity - 12 Muffins

Ingredients

1/3 Cup of Shortening
1/3 Cup of Sugar
3/4 Cup of Milk
1/2 Teaspoon of Salt
1 Cup of Flour
4 Tablespoons of Baking Powder
1 Cup of Yellow Corn Meal
1 Egg

Procedure

Cream shortening, sugar and salt. Beat egg and milk and add to above. Mix well. Mix flour and baking powder dry, add to above mixture and stir well. Add corn meal and mix lightly. Put in hot greased muffin tin, filling 3/4 full. Cook in hot oven for twenty (20) minutes.

Batter For Fruit Fritters

Formula No. 1203 • Quantity - 15 Portions, 2 Each

Ingredients

2 cups of flour
1 tablespoon of sugar
1 Teaspoon of salt
2 cups of milk
1 egg
1-1/2 teaspoon baking powder

Procedure

Blend flour, salt, sugar in bowl thoroughly. Beat eggs and milk separately and add to dry mixture slowly so as not as to form lumps. When ready to use, add baking powder and stir well. Dip in fruit rings and fry in deep fat.

P.S. The following fruits can be used:

1/2 Cooked pears
Sliced raw apples
Sliced pineapple
Split bananas
Half cooked peach
Half cooked apricot

Wheat Cake Batter

Formula No. 1204 • Quantity - 8 Portions, 3 cakes each

Ingredients

4 Cups of flour
1 tablespoon of sugar
4 Teaspoons of salt (level)
4 teaspoons baking powder (level)
4 cups of milk
2 eggs
2 Tablespoons of honey or maple syrup
2 Tablespoons melted butter

Procedure

Mix flour, salt, sugar baking powder. Beat eggs separately and add milk to eggs. Pour into dry mixture and beat well. Add honey and melted butter. Cook on hot griddle.

P.S. If mixture is made up in advance, do not add baking powder until ready to use.

Eclair and Cream Puff Dough

Formula No. 1205

Ingredients

1 Quart of Milk
4 Cups Sifted Flour
2 Cups of Lard
2 Teaspoons of Salt
2 Teaspoons of Sugar
12 to 15 Whole Eggs

Procedure

Put milk and lard in pot on range, bring to a boil, when boiling, add flour stirring constantly with wooden spoon, and allow to cook on side of range while mixing, working it until it is smooth, remove from range and add the raw eggs two at a time, work until smooth and repeat until all eggs are incorporated.

When Cream Puffs are desired, put paste in pastry bag equipped with a metal tube, form on well-greased pan in round deposits according to size desired. This paste should increase six times its size when cooked. Cook in hot oven. For Eclairs spread paste in strips 1/2 inch wide, four inches long; brush with beaten raw egg mixed with a little water. Streak with form lengthwise before cooking. This also applies to Cream Puffs.

Pie Dough

Formula No. 1206 • Quantity - Ten 8-inch pies

Ingredients

20 Cups of Flour
6 Teaspoons of Salt
3 Cups of Butter
3 Cups of Lard
2 Cups of Water (Iced)

Procedure

Cream lard and butter. Mix flour and salt. Mix the two above gently with fingers. When properly blended, without too much handling, add iced water slowly. Form in ball shape and allow to rest in refrigerator for three (3) or four (4) hours.

Tea Biscuits
(Baking Powder Biscuits)

Formula No. 1207 • Quantity - 20 Biscuits

Ingredients

4 Cups sifted flour
4 Teaspoons Baking Powder
4 Tablespoons sugar
2 Teaspoons salt
1 Cup of lard
1 Whole raw egg
1 Cup of milk

Procedure

Mix flour, baking powder, sugar, salt and sift properly mix in lard with fingers gently. When blended, beat egg and milk, add to dry, mixture, do not work to much. Roll mixture 3/4 inch thickness on flour board, cut with round biscuit cutter. Place on baking pan and cook until golden brown.

Dumplings For Fricassees and Irish Stew

Formula No. 1208 • Quantity - 24 to 28 Dumplings

Ingredients

4-1/3 Cups of Bisquick Mix
4 Eggs
2 Teaspoons of Salt
1/2 Cup of Milk
2 Tablespoons of freshly chopped Parsley
1 Gallon of Water
2 Tablespoons of Chicken Base

Procedure

Put 4 cups of Bisquick Mix in a mixing bowl, add eggs, salt, milk and parsley, and blend well; then add 1/3 cup of Bisquick Mix to bind mixture.

To cook, set water and Chicken Base to boil. When boiling, drop dumplings in using a basting spoon 1/3 full per Dumpling.

Be sure Dumplings are done through.

Dwight Jones

The Chesapeake & Ohio Historical Society owns, as part of its historic passenger car fleet, former C&O Dining Car 965 — *Gadsby's Tavern*.

Built in 1922 by Pullman for C&O, 965 was used on the railway's mainline passenger trains. In 1932, C&O had the car— along with two sister diners from the same 1922 order— rebuilt for service on its new premier passenger train *The George Washington*. The rebuild included installation of air-conditioning as well as new interior finish and appointments to carry forth the colonial theme of the new train. Additionally, each of the dining cars bore the name of a colonial tavern which had significance in Washington's life.

The car remained in service on the C&O, with little modification, until 1953 when it was modernized by the railway to continue operation on its mainline passenger trains. Finally in 1967, due to declining demand for passenger trains, C&O declared the car surplus and it was sold to a private owner.

Having had several owners in the intervening years, the car was purchased by the C&O Historical Society in 1985 with funds contributed by individuals and corporate sponsors for that specific purpose. The car retained most of its original interior fixtures in the dining room, but its original kitchen equipment had been removed and the car had suffered from corrosion damage and neglect. After years of hard work and dedication by several C&OHS members and with the support of many other individuals, members and organizations, the car was restored to its approximate 1932 appearance and returned to service as a railroad dining car on special excursion trains during 1993. When not being used on special trains or excursion service, the car is based in Clifton Forge, Virginia.

Gadsby's Tavern provides the C&OHS a unique opportunity to interpret the history of C&O's rich and colorful dining car service and it is especially fitting that this car — the only known survivor of the original *George Washington* train — be the venue in which to accomplish that purpose.

George Washington's Railroad
CHESAPEAKE and OHIO
Lines
Original Predecessor Company Founded by George Washington in 1784